BREAKING
THE
GOOD MOM
MYTH

BREAKING THE
GOOD MOM
MYTH

*Every Modern Mom's Guide to
Getting Past Perfection, Regaining Sanity,
and Raising Great Kids*

ALYSON SCHAFER

Collins

Breaking the Good Mom Myth
Copyright © 2009 by Alyson Schafer.

Published by Collins, an imprint of HarperCollins Publishers Ltd

Originally published by John Wiley & Sons Canada, Ltd.: 2012
First published by HarperCollins Publishers Ltd in an EPub edition: 2013
This Collins trade paperback edition: 2014

HarperCollins books may be purchased for educational, business, or sales
promotional use through our Special Markets Department.

HarperCollins Publishers Ltd
2 Bloor Street East, 20th Floor
Toronto, Ontario, Canada
M4W 1A8

www.harpercollins.ca

Library and Archives Canada Cataloguing in Publication
information is available upon request.

ISBN 978-1-44342-767-8

Printed and bound in the United States of America
RRD 9 8 7 6 5 4 3 2 1

DEDICATION

To my family; Ken, Zoe and Lucy, who were as excited
about this book project as I was. They gave me up to the world
of writing with blessings. I am truly grateful.

And to my mother, Sylvia Knight, who truly knew the art of
encouraging children.

TABLE OF CONTENTS

INTRODUCTION
TODAY'S GOOD MOTHER

> *I am a competent person—I want to get this right.*

I don't know anyone who has embarked on the journey of motherhood and hasn't at some point felt overwhelmed by the job. We're often embarrassed to admit it, even to each other, preferring instead to suffer privately with our feelings of guilt and panicked moments when we lose confidence in what we are doing. At times we feel judged and utterly out of control. It can be a truly horrid place to be.

Good moms like us, well, we just can't seem to cut ourselves any slack! We come down hard on ourselves, thinking we're screwing it up and convinced we're on the verge of emotionally scarring our children. Under all this pressure, we wind up doing the very things we swore we'd never do in our parenting, and we're left to wonder: What happened to all the fantasies I had about being a mother?

No matter how hard we try (and, oh, how we *do* try!) to get to everything we're supposed to be doing and to do it all well, it just feels like it's a near impossible task. Yet we're convinced others are doing it, making it, hitting the mark. So why can't we? What's wrong with us? Our solution: push ever harder, hoping that somehow, with more effort we'll get it "right." But have you noticed that we never seem to get there? We never seem to arrive, kick back, relax, and allow ourselves to simply enjoy motherhood. We never get to perfect.

Contemporary parenting is fraught with worry and anxiety, isolation and performance pressure. Yet, one of the most pervasive cultural myths of our time is that we're meant to be totally enjoying it. After all, becoming a mother is what many of us have pined for since we dragged our dollies around with us as little girls. So now "real" motherhood is here, and it's supposed to be the best thing that ever happened to us, right?

Ah, motherhood—this is fun, right?

I don't think it helps matters that our generation is coming into motherhood at a time in parenting history when our culture wholeheartedly believes that children are ever-so-fragile and utterly dependent. We feel that whatever happens to them is on *our* shoulders. We have taken on the entire responsibility for how our children's lives evolve, and that's a BIG deal! We're near paralyzed by the fear that we simply can't afford to slip up. We're told that what we do as mothers will forever cast their future. How do you like having that responsibility?

So, what do we do? We take on childrearing with the same driven attitude and perfectionism that our achievement-oriented, competitive culture espouses for seemingly every task these days, from education and careers to driving, cooking, and sure, why not go for your black belt in yoga while we're being ludicrous? "Competitive peacefulness." Wow—this is a sign of how far off the mark we've come!

Parenting has become a competitive pursuit, and it's fuelled by a child-focused culture that has put our children on a precious pedestal. We've lifted childrearing to new heights. This is no longer an intuitive job for the masses. No. It apparently requires resources, research, and skills training to "execute." Seems we're now in the *business* of "people-building" and "unlocking potentials," and frankly, it's starting to look a lot more like project management than parenting, with our kids becoming the measure of our mothering success. Yech! The trouble is, our own self-worth is so tied to it all that we can't seem to let go of it, even when we know better. Let's face it—deep inside we abide by the belief that if we fail motherhood, it will be our *ultimate* failure and, alternately, if our children "work out," it's our crowning accomplishment. Isn't it? Are we courageous enough to admit it?

So how do we know if we are "doing it right," "being successful?"

> *How do you know if you are a "good mother?"*

We're obsessed with knowing, so we read, research, measure, judge, compare, compete, and perform. We have to, because we believe that if *we* aren't perfect, it's our kids who will pay the price for our mistakes. That is the big, ugly burden we carry.

So... it's off to soccer practice, Kumon Math, piano lessons (which they hate, but playing an instrument is vital), and don't forget to stop at the Montessori school to drop off the pre-registration for the baby (yes, he's only three months old now, but you *know* how long those waiting lists are for good schools). Be sure you're leaving time to squeeze in a Pilates class so you can be both a centred and sexy "yummy mummy." Jump in the leased minivan you can't really afford (but how ya gonna live with one car on this schedule?) to catch the infant stimulation and baby salsa classes at the neighborhood birth and pregnancy center, call the doula, pose for a belly cast, and then zoom home to help with (translation: *fight over*) homework. Dinner needs consideration; you must make something balanced and healthy, with no saturated fats. Remember to rinse off trace pesticide residues and watch milk for growth hormones and—oh my, you didn't just serve tap water did you?

When did neurotic become normal?

> *"It's no measure of health to be well adjusted to a profoundly sick society."*
>
> —Jiddu Krishnamurti

Come on! Is this *really* what we've gotta do in order to be a good mother in this day and age? Have we all drunk the toxic Kool-Aid? Society has sold us iconic images of the "good mother," and the effort we put into reaching these ideals is not only misguided, it's detrimental to family life, as we'll see in the pages ahead.

If you stop and think about it, the "good mother" ideal is about as ridiculous as the Barbie doll beauty ideal. We've all heard that if Barbie were a live woman, her dimensions would put her at seven feet tall with a 40-inch chest and an 18-inch waist. Well, I believe if an iconic good mother *really* existed, she would have to have six arms, four hips, and be so highly evolved that her nipples would be conveniently located on her ankles, making them 100 percent accessible for her crawling babe. She would never need sleep, always be happy and patient, be equally adept at coaching soccer and helping with trigonometry homework, be able to co-exist in three places at once, and have $100K in disposable cash to spend on herself and the kids. C'mon—do you wanna look like that? (I know, except for the nipples, it actually sounds not bad.)

The point is, these good mother icons are nothing more than modern-day myths, and they're making us miserable! These myths create a monolithic story, telling us how we should be and what we should be doing in order to be a good mother. We already have our own private, idiosyncratic confabulations about how to be a good mother, but we also have to navigate the greater societal myths of "good motherhood."

HOW DID WE GET SO CRAZY?

It wasn't always this hard to hit the good mother mark. In earlier times we had tremendous faith in children, believing they would develop just fine, with minimal interference required. We treated children as robust and capable, and were aware that they could manage life. We made demands on them, and we expected them to adapt and accommodate as needed. They weren't thought of as so precious and vulnerable back then. Nor did we carry the sole burden of "making or breaking" our children. Previous generations had the benefit of sharing the load. "It takes a village to raise a child," as the saying goes, and we used to act more like a united village. Historically, there was a singular dominant ideal—one prevailing cultural myth—that dictated what the good mother was to do, so it looked pretty much the same in every household. If you saw a child misbehaving in the park, you took matters into your own hands because everyone dealt with kids more or less the same way. Image that happening these days? We'd be apoplectic at the thought of disciplining a stranger's child.

So that makes for a bit of a dilemma. Today we suffer the burden of wanting to be good mothers, but without understanding exactly what that means. Everyone has a different idea of what is "right." Do you go back to work, or not? Do you immunize, or not? Do you share a family bed, or not? Do you offer a pacifier, or not? Do you buy the $300 titanium helmet—or do you not quite love your child *that* much? Ouch! Mothers today don't have clear marching orders. Instead, we're faced with a barrage of instructions, often in direct conflict with each other.

This means we are no longer a homogenous community of moms. Instead, we are mothering "factions" split into opposing camps. No universal support means we can easily feel as though we're under attack for our choices by mothers who are not like-minded. The working moms and the stay-at-home moms eye each other with envy but also with judgment, and the further apart we get from each other, the harder it becomes for any of us to make these tough decisions.

DOES ANYONE HAVE THE ANSWERS?

Part of the reason we feel lost and confused is that it's not just our peers we've tuned out, but also the supposed experts who in the past gave us calm reassurances. Not anymore. We no longer trust our institutions and their "authoritative" answers. We live in an information age, so when our doctor offers a prescription, we don't just accept their script and start serving up pills to our tots. No. Instead we hurry on home to do our *own* primary research, only to be deluged with conflicting opinions. Who's right? Whose advice do we follow? What if we get it wrong?

As the ultimate decision maker for our children, we feel the only solution is to gain our *own* mastery in an ever-growing number of domains: everything from how to treat an ear infection right down to the biochemistry of Tupperware at various heating points, and so on and so forth, ad infinitum. And who benefits? Well, let's just remember that worry sells, and mothers spend billions annually calming that worry.

I just want to be a good mother—tell me how, and I'll do it!

Can you relate to all of this? Have I painted a picture that captures the essence of our mothering mania, the ride we all want to get off of?

As a therapist and coach, I have worked with a great many mothers who have found tremendous relief in giving up the Good Mom myth. It doesn't mean you blow off motherhood and childrearing or any other backlash response. Instead, this book is a chance to explore a new way of thinking. It's a chance to open our eyes to a new and positive framework for building loving families, to learn how people grow, develop, and relate with one another. Don't worry—there will also be sex, intrigue, power struggles, tantrums, hair-brained husbands, and battering siblings; it's not just a psychology book! I will show you the myths that bring our families unneeded troubles, and pragmatic techniques for doing things differently that you can try out immediately.

We're going to be undoing some of your early programming, so cut yourself some slack! Don't be afraid to have a laugh. I'm going to tease you and motherhood in the chapters to come, not to be mean, but to remind all of us to keep the weight of this as light as possible. THAT is the attitude that best supports change and growth. And with that attitude in place, we'll learn to hang onto the aspects of our mothering that are working well, and to carefully discard anything that hinders us from what we really need to be doing: raising great kids and enjoying our families!

CHAPTER 1

MYTH:
SELF-CARE IS SELFISH

W hen was the last time you went to the bathroom alone? Ate a meal without a child on your lap? Had an uninterrupted night's sleep or were called something other than "Ryan's mom"?

We've been raised to believe the myth that "good mothers" always put their children first. We feel guilty if we attend to our own needs, believing we're being selfish if we aren't fully concentrating on our children.

Such was the case with Mary—and a million other moms out there just like her. I hope you're reading this, Mary. Do you remember talking to me? I met you after I spoke at your mothers group. You and I grabbed a corner and had our coffee together. In our brief, yet intense, conversation I could hear your exasperation and exhaustion. I could tell you were really giving it your all to be a "good mom." What you wouldn't do for your kids! I could tell your children were your life. Their needs always came first. Mary, you took this business of motherhood seriously. But it was also very clear to me—you were totally spent.

So for the moms like Mary, I am starting this myth-busting journey with the topic of YOU and how you treat yourself. You see, I meet a lot of moms like Mary through my courses and coaching practice. They secure my services for a variety of reasons: How can I get my kids to listen, to stop tantrumming? How can I get my toddler to eat, or get my kids to stop fighting with each other? They want advice on parenting practices. They want their home life to be better.

I want to offer up quick help to these moms, but how can I give them new parenting techniques to implement when it looks like these mothers are on the very edge of collapse and would crumple under a feather! Is that you, too? Do you feel weepy some days? Or short-tempered? Did your behavior during the infamous "chucked-sippy-cup-to-the-head-while-driving incident" of last Tuesday have you thinking you should take an anger management course—or else seek a career as a prison guard in a men's penitentiary? How much evidence do I need to show moms that they parent more effectively when they are not near collapse?

Yes, it takes energy and courage to change the dynamics of our families. We have much exciting work ahead of us in the chapters to come, but we have to start with first things first: If you want to implement change in your families, if you want to have parenting success, we have to find ways of rejuvenating YOU so we can get you back into the game. Who knew giving up perfection would actually require energy? Yup, we have work to do, people!

When I made the slightest mention of what Mary might do for herself, Mary clammed up. The mere idea of taking time to rejuvenate was seen as sacrilege. Mary, I thought I was throwing you a lifeline, but you didn't seem to want to grab it.

How about you? Do you always put your kids and family first and leave your own needs last—or perhaps unmet? Answer *true* or *false* to the following:

1. Your husband plays golf every weekend, but you wouldn't even think of asking him to watch the kids while you went out antiquing or for brunch with friends. You don't want to impose on others for your recreation. It's not like you *have* to go after all.

2. You make sure your kids have regular haircuts, dental appointments, annual checkups, and eye exams—but you don't do the same for yourself.

3. You don't prepare your favorite dishes because the others don't really like them. Instead you forfeit your wishes to suit the rest of the family; chicken nuggets, hot dogs, and—yee haw, grilled cheese … again. What ever happened to salmon, pesto, and curries?

4. You get up every night with the baby who cries like clockwork for a bottle at 3 a.m. You figure it's just as much hassle to wake your husband as it is to go to the baby yourself.

5. Your life seems busier than ever, but it also seems to be shrinking in scope. The only aspect of your life getting any attention is work and dealing with running the family. Hobbies are nonexistent, friendships left fallow, community and volunteer work avoided, and you haven't crossed the threshold of your church or temple in as long as you can remember.

6. You feel guilty outsourcing anything you could do yourself, since it could save the family a few bucks if you groomed the dog yourself, steam-cleaned the carpets yourself, cleaned the house instead of hiring a cleaning service, ironed shirts instead of dry-cleaning ...

7. You're addicted to the adrenaline rush you're on. When you stop, you crash and need a venti caramel latte to get through the afternoon, then a big glass of merlot to de-stress at the end of the day.

8. You're just not happy and you can't seem to put your finger on why.

9. You bought this book, but you feel badly about spending the money on yourself, and you're still not sure when you'll find the time to read it. Congrats for getting this far! Seems you've already managed to claim some time for yourself. BRAVA!

How did you do? It's hard to look after our own needs when our culture so reveres the acts of self-sacrificing mothers. Just watch the admiring expressions on people's faces when they hear the family folklores of how Grandma "never bought anything for herself," how she "always made sure the children had enough," and how she often "went without" to provide for them.

Awwww!!! Everybody together now—let's make one unified sigh of admiration. WOW—What a gooooood mother!

Apparently, wiping our children's snotty noses on our own sleeve is a good thing, while saying, "Oh gross—get a Kleenex" is somehow less loving.

Well, the myth-busting begins here ladies. We need to re-examine the heroic and saintly status we bestow on that iconic selfless "good mother" who lives her life for her kids, subverting her own needs, and risks losing her own sense of self. We've worked so hard to throw off our aprons, burn our bras, and get educated. We've been trying to get out of being second-class citizens, but when bassinettes and bibs come onto the scene, we find ourselves back at the old gender formula. Seems our mommy myths missed the revolution! Sure a new baby needs to be tended to, and will require huge amounts of our time and energy. That's even MORE reason to care for yourself.

Even with the benefits of the feminist movement, there are still culturally entrenched gender issues at play here. Being a successful *man* requires being a "protector and provider" to the family. The masculine ideal is still tied to being the breadwinner and gaining success in the workforce. While the majority of women do have careers outside the home—in order to reach the feminine ideal, women are ultimately required to be successful at the job of looking after the babies.

We're doing double duty and run ragged, yet we believe we're supposed to be able to do this mothering thing in a seemingly tireless and stress-free way. If we're taxed physically or emotionally, we see it as a mark of failure.

What do you mean you don't you want to be with them at every waking moment? Isn't playing with trucks all day fulfilling enough for you? Why isn't making play-dough sculptures stimulating your middle-aged mind? Are you bent? What else do you need, women? Why do you need to get away? Why do you need something more? Isn't this what you're *supposed* to be doing and loving? How come you don't seem to be coping? Other moms seem to be able to find time to shower and dress, why are you still in your pajamas at 11 a.m.? How come you're choking back tears? You're loving this time of your life, right? Who wouldn't wanna be with kids all day baking cookies. *What's your problem?*

What's your problem? You are dying on the vine! Name it, claim it—and let's do something about it!

LESSONS FROM AIRLINES

When you're dying on the vine of your own life, you gotta take the advice from the airlines. I know Air Canada is not your usual source of mothering wisdom, but they make a good point that bears repeating here.

The airline gives the following instructions: "If the cabin pressure should fall, an air mask will drop from the compartment above. Parents should secure their own air masks first and then secure their children's."

Now why do you figure they say that? Do you think the airlines care *less* about children and want them to get their oxygen last? NO! Of course not. They know that you're no good as a caregiver to your children if you're not first cared for yourself. By taking care of yourself, are you being selfish or responsible?

If being selfish is defined as engaging in activities that serve to benefit only you, with no regard for how your actions affect others, then I agree—being selfish is not good. But the acts of self-care that I'm trying to get mothers to adopt are not self-serving.

Self-care is NOT selfish— it benefits the whole family.

SELF-CARE IS **NOT** SELFISH

Every person needs self-care as an essential ingredient for effective living—*especially* if you're a mother with dependants counting on you. I'm going to offer you this new, healthy myth to consider adopting: Good mothers respect themselves and care for themselves as a part of responsible and effective parenting.

Let's see if we can coach you through some change in this chapter. Once you begin looking after yourself, you'll be ready to tackle all the changes that you would like to embrace in the chapters ahead. You'll learn to stop striving towards being a "good mother" and instead begin to truly enjoy the fruits of building a fulfilling family life through effective parenting with intentionality. You'll be at peace with human imperfection and embrace yourself for doing what you can at the moment, instead of railing yourself for being a failure at hitting motherly perfection. (Hopefully, you'll scoff at the very idea of perfection when we conclude this book!)

Perhaps you're already doing some things to look after yourself, but you find that even with attempts to treat yourself well your battery just keeps draining more and more quickly. Are you starting to find that all the pedicures in the world aren't going to cheer you up?

We're a culture in love with putting band-aids on symptoms. Self-care needs to take on a wider meaning in our society. We need "meta-self-care." Meta-self-care means recognizing that mothers, like everyone else, need to feel personally satisfied in their own lives and feel good living in their own skin.

Tending to children may be your life ambition and you may find it a joy, but you are a whole person and a human, not a mother machine. We need enrichment too, and we can get it through diverse means. We have other relationships and roles, desires and aspirations. Attending to the whole of our person doesn't make us *less* of a mother, or *less* loving of our children. It doesn't diminish our mothering if we also celebrate and enjoy being a wife, a sister, a friend, a community member, a professional, and more. Life is rich and complex. You can choose to relish that diversity instead of feeling pulled in all directions and disloyal to your children.

This is not an added burden! It's about seeing a larger context for our lives. We need to look through a more panoramic lens on our life in its entirety. When we're caring for ourselves and our relationships, embracing our core values, and living with intention, we can actually lead our families in a much more meaningful and energetic way.

Do you deny yourself the profound pleasures of life in the hopes that they are banked somewhere, to be withdrawn later? Do you just *manage* to get by? Or are you leading the way toward joyfulness? I find that mothers who simply manage their families are more apt to burn out. Mothers who manage (and often beautifully, I might add) can't seem to see the forest for the trees. It isn't enough to be well rested and yogafied with nice nails. We need to have a purpose and be fulfilled. Could it be you are running your life beautifully—but it just isn't the life you'd like to be leading?

Bridgette decided while on mat leave that she didn't want to return to work—but she also felt she needed more than just 24/7 mothering. She was a marketing exec and decided to start an online newsletter for moms. Bridgette became a mom-prenuer and combined her joys to make a balance of all she wanted in her life. Yes, she worked hard around the clock and had to juggle more balls, but her happiness of living the life she wanted was a wellspring of energy that kept her happy and charged up. She has less money, less time, less sleep, and yet she could tell she was a better mother when she was happy and loving her life.

What is it that YOU need to be doing—not only to sustain yourself, but indeed to enrich yourself so that you're living the life you want to be living? Have you let the tail wag the dog long enough? Many mothers begin to reconsider what they want from life when they start a family. It is a new chapter in your life, a change and new start. You may find your values and priorities have changed. Here's the bottom line: Happy mothers lead happy families! Investing in you spills over to the whole family. It starts with you! This can be an exciting time of awakening for mothers. We have an opportunity to stop and take stock of our values, to decide consciously about the life we would like to make for ourselves and our families.

WHY SELF-CARE IS IMPORTANT

Can you see from Bridgette's story the reasons putting yourself *first* instead of *last* is important? Let's look at the top five reasons.

1. You Need to Be Healthy and Alive

Research has shown that stress compromises the body's immune system and makes you way more susceptible to disease. Chronic stress will shorten your life expectancy. Don't die early of a stress-induced heart attack! Stressed-out people are also more prone to accidents, and given that motor vehicle accidents are a leading killer in childhood, you need to be able to achieve calm, focused attention—if only for safety reasons!

If you had to be replaced, would you hire someone like yourself—in your current shape—to care for your own children?

2. You Need to Be at Your Best to Give Them Your Best

Bubble baths and trips to the gym won't melt your stress if you're unhappy with your current life situation. Learn about yourself, discover what's important for you, and go about getting it in place in your life so you feel fulfilled. Self-help books, coaching, and counseling can all help you get the big picture sorted out for yourself. For some mothers that means going back to work. For others it means leaving work. For some it means hiring a live-in nanny, and for others it's the painful decision to ask your mother-in-law to please go home. The point is that there is no one perfect formula for motherly happiness. You have to decide for yourself what you authentically need to be fulfilled. We need to be quiet and listen to ourselves. We need to shut up that chorus of voices in our heads that tell us what our husbands think is best, what our parents want for us, what our friends will say about any change we make. You have to listen very hard to find your OWN voice in all of that, but trust that your heart knows the answers to what you desire, to what you need. Give yourself permission and have the courage to make it happen. GO FOR IT!

3. You Set the Tone
Moms and dads are the captains of the family ship. They drive and direct the whole family system. It makes perfect sense to keep your leaders clear-headed and content so they can lead properly. If parents are happy, patient, and loving, that will create the tone for your whole home. Alternatively, misery loves company. If mom is moody and short-tempered, the entire house will follow in kind.

4. You Set an Example
What do you want your children to learn about the nature and role of women and mothers? Will you perpetuate the long-held myth of inequity that places women and mothers in a position of servitude and selflessness, belittling our true power and worth? Or will you model a 21st-century enlightened women who acts in self-respecting ways and leads her life as a full person? You help

meld your children's attitudes about gender equality and human relationships. What they experience watching you function in your role contributes to the ideas of the kind of wife and mother they will aspire to be or have in their life one day, too.

5. You Are Able to Be Proactive
We acclimate to stress and become impervious to our internal state until we're spent and bankrupt, and then we retreat to our old known ways and comfort zones. Just as a stretched elastic will recoil into its original shape, so too do we fall back into our non-thinking, knee-jerk, reflex-triggered parenting that usually is *not* the way we prefer to parent. It takes energy and focused attention to be proactive instead of reactive. We can only be proactive when our reserves are filled.

SO WHY DON'T WE TAKE CARE OF OURSELVES?

Top Lame Reasons for Not Taking Time for Yourself
1. *"I work full-time and can't squeeze in another single thing."*
2. *"I just don't feel right spending money on me, ever since I stopped earning my own salary."*
3. *"I don't have childcare."*
4. *"My husband can't manage the kids on his own."*
5. *"How would I get there? We're a one-car family."*
6. *"I don't even know what I'd do."*
7. *"I don't have the energy."*

I know, I know—and you probably have a hangnail too. Poor you. You just can't change your ways, eh? Let me tell you, I could lend you money, rent you a car, and watch your children, and for some of you it still wouldn't do the trick. You know why? Because, like Mary from the moms' group, you're still holding the myth that severe selflessness is actually a *good* thing. It's what you feel *makes* you a good mother. You're not going to pursue activities that you feel will lower your good mother status. We gotta bust the myth in order to get change to occur. In such cases, we therapists like to do something called "spitting in the client's soup." Sound gross? Good—it's supposed to. Here's how it works.

Spitting in the Client's Soup
If I were to lean over and spit into the bowl of soup you were enjoying, you'd be in a dilemma. You liked the soup, but now it's been soured by spit. You could either stop eating, or sure, you could still eat the soup, but it would not taste as good to you. Similarly, a therapist can find ways to make the behaviors that clients engage in less "palatable" by souring the experience for them. We do this by revealing *why* they behave in a certain way, by informing them of the payoff they receive for that behavior. Most people don't like the answer, but they usually agree with it. The client may choose to continue the behavior, but it will never be as enjoyable, since they are now aware of the payoff or motivation, and that realization is souring to know.

Here's why behaving in such "good motherly ways of selflessness" should "taste bad" to you: Selflessness is not selfless at all—it's all about being superior. Let me show you how.

Selflessness Is Really About Superiority
All behavior serves a purpose, and our "selflessness" is useful in that martyrdom (yes, that's what it is, plain and simple) acts to elevate our status. The most selfless mother is the most superior mother! HA! There's a twist for your brain. Turns out that this is really all about our personal ego, status, and superiority over others and not goodwill toward our children, as we would have ourselves believe.

That means, if I suggest self-care to Mary and she holds the belief that "good mothers" are selfless and put their children first, then according to her myth, attending to herself would mean lowering her good mother status. It plain won't happen! Not until we bust the myth. So what do you think? Are selfless martyrs superior to others? Does selflessness make you "above" others? Does it make you a superior person? Is "Martyr Mary" superior as a human being to mom-prenuer Brigette who had the audacity to start a business for her own pleasure even though her child will have less of her mom's time?

If we reject the whole good-better-best way of thinking about people and their worth and instead get on with doing what needs to be done, we can see that we really do need to be taking care of ourselves and we need not have worries about these fictional "status" issues.

I hope the next time you find yourself saying, "Sure we can go to the park—let me just take three Advils for this crushing headache, I don't want you to miss out on your fun just because I may be having an aneurysm," that maybe you'll catch yourself and realize just how silly and superior that is! Repeat after me: "NO—I am sorry, I can't do the park today. I don't feel well enough." Hey, not bad! I think you're gonna do just fine with this! Unless, of course, you lie in bed with your headache but you feel guilty now...

Guilt Feelings

Ah, good ol' guilt feelings. Here is some more "spitting in your soup" for you. Once you learn about guilt and how it works, you're never going to enjoy the benefits of feeling guilty again. Sorry to spoil that for you. You see, guilt can be thought of as "good intentions we don't intend to keep." Let me explain further for you. By feeling guilty we allow ourselves to maintain our superior "good mother" status without having to actually change our behavior. What a coup! Act badly, feel guilty, and still keep a high status. Sounds too good to be true, doesn't it? Our guilt implies that we know better and should be judged favorably for that "knowing" alone.

So if you feel guilty for not going to the park, you are saying, "Good mothers would go to the park. I am not doing that, but because I feel guilty about it, it shows that I *know* that I should, so I am still a good mother. Now I get to have my cake and eat it, too—I get to *not* go to the park and I don't have to feel like a bad mother, because I am feeling guilty about it! Instead, why not:

1. Don't feel guilty—having a headache it is a legitimate reason to stay home.
2. Don't feel guilty—if you don't think a headache is reason to stay home from the park, then go to the park!

Either way, you don't have to feel guilty. Next time you feel guilty, ask yourself what you're giving yourself permission to do or not do and then think of how you feel your status is threatened in some way.

The "Woulda-Coulda-Shoulda-Oughta" Dilemma

Of course, there's always the fear that moms will now add "self-care" to their growing list of things they "oughta" be doing. Creeakkkk—what's that sound? Is it the sound of the bar being raised just that little bit higher? Do you feel like I'm raising expectations even further? Hey, I don't want moms to fall into the mental trap of what I call the "woulda, coulda, shoulda, oughtas." Oh, how easy it is to bash ourselves, feeling badly about all the many things we "woulda, coulda, shoulda, oughta" be doing to be good mothers:

- *Woulda* gone out for a jog last night if dinner wasn't so late.

- *Coulda* found a book club if I woulda just asked around more.
- *Shoulda* found a babysitter way before now.
- *Oughta* get a weekend away with my girlfriend soon.

That kind of thinking simply furthers our frustrations and continues to make us feel we are falling short of the good mother mark. We must work to keep ourselves out of this kind of discouraging and self-defeating thinking. Good mother expectations are no help to us. They are nothing but a load to bear and they drag us down. We've got to decide that it's time to drop the load!

The idea of meta-self-care is to invest in rejuvenating oneself. It isn't supposed to be a burden. That's missing the entire point! Don't add "self-care" to your list of things you need to be doing to be a stupendously good mother, a list that allows you to measure how you are doing and that you can ceremoniously tick off:

- Yoga—done
- Daily soy beverage and omega 3-6-9's—done
- Weekly mani-pedi—done
- Read fabulous book by renowned author—done
- Support the arts—done
- Create a legacy—done

Oh, we are so damn fabulous! But I promise we're not deeply happy if we take the tickbox approach. To ensure we don't go the route of scratching things off of the shoulda, woulda, coulda, oughta list, simply ask yourself the following question about your choice of self-care: "Do I feel good *while* I am doing yoga? Or running? Or hosting this luncheon? Or only after it's done and behind me?"

If you feel good while you are in the process, that is the ticket! You're onto something here. The task is rejuvenating. If you only feel good after the fact, when you can tick it off your list, chances are you're not really rejuvenating yourself, but feeling satisfied that you've been doing what you "should be" doing. There is a world of difference.

We're looking for activities that energize you, things that you look forward to, race out of the house for. This should be something that you anticipate with joy and revel in while you're doing it. That means you no longer get to consider doing grocery shopping and errands without kids in tow as self-care! Okay?

What is it for you? Working in a community garden? Drawing? Going to an art gallery? Taking your Labrador to the senior centre for the "canine friendly" visiting program? Renovating a bathroom? Bird watching? Cooking? Watching soap operas? Curling? Journaling? Walking the dog? Being a reading buddy at the school? Singing? Learning belly dancing? Glass blowing, taking an online course, learning cake decorating? What is it for you?

Stop thinking of all the reasons you can't do this and think outside the box to figure out ways you CAN! We're so quick to shut ourselves down without even looking for possible solutions to logistics of it all. But I have seen many a happy mother work it through for themselves. You can, too! Honest.

Marg, Carol, and Vanessa created a childcare pool. Each mom takes a turn watching the others' kids so one mom can get out on her own.

Jim and Sally decided to sell their house and move onto their beloved sailboat with their daughter Gillian. Not everyone would make this decision—but their hearts are in sailing, and without a mortgage to carry, they had less financial stress and more time to sail!

CHANGE CAN START WITH A SIMPLE EXPERIMENT

Sylvie was a working mom who had a challenging daughter. She complained that she was just too tired to put up with these antics anymore. Every day was a fight from sunup to sundown. She was throwing in the towel.

When I asked Sylvie what she did in her non-mothering time, she said there was none. Her daughter and her career were full-time jobs. I asked her what she *would* do if she had time for other things. She drew a blank. When I initially invited her to take some time to develop some outside hobbies, she gave me a lot of pushback: "I am too tired to do more. There is no free time, we can't afford any other expenses," and so on and so forth. The rationalizing of all the reasons she couldn't care for herself went on and on. We finally came up with one small idea, that on the next Sunday morning she would make arrangements to go sit in a big lounge chair at the local Starbucks and read the Sunday paper, cover to cover, in peace. That was the only commitment I could get her to make. Even that took my badgering her to make this seemingly huge imposition on her family (all two hours and $5 worth of it). The only way I could get her to give it a whirl was to position it as a one-time experiment. This was her "coaching homework" and she was to report on it. It took a lot for her to ask her family for this time for herself.

Guess what? They were happy to oblige. Dad and daughter looked forward to enjoying this time at home alone together. That first Sunday, Sylvie discovered that not only did she love this experience, but when she came home, her whole afternoon with her daughter went better. Everyone actually seemed happier. This was a small first step, but after experiencing the positive outcome for everyone, she went on to make a bunch of changes in her life. She got the creative idea (and nerve) to ask her employer if she could work flex hours to take some of the stress off her schedule, and he agreed. Next she enrolled in a water-color painting class, even though it meant being out of the house one night a week and her husband having to cut work short to come home and look after dinner. She would never have imposed this way in the past. But once she experienced all the secondary benefits to her own happiness, she realized the family *did* run more harmoniously when she was happy. I spoke with Sylvie recently and she is looking into going back to school for a fine arts degree. Go figure.

So, how about it? Are YOU ready to make some changes yourself? Do you already know what you need to do for yourself? If you do—go for it! If you are unsure of how this might all look in your own life, why not check out the self-help section of the library and look for coaching books that include a workbook section. Reading, coaching, counseling—whatever resources you engage, the important idea is to value yourself. This is your invitation to respect yourself and your very real needs. As a mental health practitioner I urge you to rejuvenate yourself and find your own happiness so that you can be ready and eager to tackle the work of motherhood!

CHAPTER 2

MYTH:
MY CHILDREN ARE A REFLECTION OF ME

On Children

And a woman who held a babe against her bosom said, "Speak to us of Children." And he said:
Your children are not your children.
They are the sons and daughters of Life's longing for itself.
They come through you but not from you,
And though they are with you, yet they belong not to you.
You may give them your love but not your thoughts.
For they have their own thoughts.
You may house their bodies but not their souls,
For their souls dwell in the house of tomorrow, which you cannot visit, not even in your dreams.

—*Kahlil Gibran*

What a powerful and ultimately truthful sentiment. But c'mon, let's face it—it's very hard to be philosophical when it's *your* kid who's the terror of the ball pit at McDonald's. When your version of "Life's longing for itself" has just shoved a stranger's now-screaming toddler onto the floor, it tends to feel rather clear that your children ARE your children.

Besides, as much as we adore him, Kahlil was likely at home writing poetry while Mrs. Gibran faced society's parenting scrutiny, worrying everyone was judging her as a mother because of Kahlil Junior's untied sandal straps.

What a burden to carry. We feel our children are a reflection of how we are doing as mothers. If they look good, we look good. If they look bad, we look bad. And, lord knows, "good mothers" are not allowed to look bad!

Each and every one of us has had a moment when we've thought to ourselves, "What kind of mother will people think I am?" We'll do nearly anything to stop misbehavior and save face at that moment, and that leads to ineffective parenting. When we become consumed with how we look as mothers, we easily lose track of the type of guidance our children need.

In this chapter we're going to tackle the whole notion of judging people and their worth. We'll look closer at these little human beings and how they develop from a psychological perspective, and I'll pitch you my style of slow parenting, with the hopes that you'll get in the game with me. We're going to make the big move away from "good mothering" and the pitfalls of perfectionism, and move towards "effective parenting" instead. I'll also reveal the real reasons behind children's misbehavior. No, you're not the "cause" of bad behavior the way you might think. We'll start building your ability to trust yourself to parent effectively, without needless worry about others' opinions, and especially without beating yourself up.

CHILDREN AS CHATTEL

When we believe the myth that our children are a reflection of us, we end up treating them as chattel, as possessions that affect our worth in some way. No pressure here, eh kids? This means you're allowing your value as a person to be predicated on the actions of another human being. This is problematic. In fact, the widely held myth that our children are reflections of us has led to widespread parenting behaviors so extreme that recommendations have been made to create a new psychiatric diagnosis called Achievement by Proxy Syndrome, as parents become pathologically pushy, raising "trophy" kids. This myth has also necessitated the creation of a new specialty in pediatric sports medicine to deal with the huge spike in childhood injuries—injuries that are the result of parents and other adult role models pushing children too hard for their growing bodies, knowing the child's success makes them look good.

Socially, we tend to accept the notion of separating the deed from the doer when it comes to how we view our children—"I love you; it's your behavior I don't like"—but we don't apply this basic and valuable lesson to ourselves. How about it, mom, can you detangle your worth from your mothering, and from your child's behavior? Hard, isn't it?

We're so eager to take the blame and to bask in the credit. Are our children simply "the product" we good mothers are manufacturing? Are human babies nothing more than lumps of clay we mold to our liking? I don't think we really believe that. So, why do we act as if we are the artists solely responsible for their creation? Talk about robbing our children of their own merit. (Talk about encouraging misbehavior!) And, reciprocally then, if things are going wrong with our children, is it right that we take the whole blame and give no sense of accountability to the child?

So just what is your child's role in all this? We have to honor that our children are creative beings, making their *own* decisions and interpretations of life. They experience life through their own lens, a unique, subjective perception. With every passing event, they are shaping their ideas about themselves and the world and how they best fit into it. They are myth-making, too. They are devising their own stories and cautionary tales that will give them rules and instructions about how to operate in life. This is called their "lifestyle," which is akin to personality, and it is formulated by the time they are about four to six years old. It is their characteristic patterns of beliefs, and these influence behavior. Yes—we definitely have an influence, but there are limits to our influence and we must be willing to accept that other factors *beyond us* shape our children. They decide for themselves what to take note of, who they view as significant, and what rules of living they are creating for themselves. Sometimes, those beliefs and self-created rules lead to misbehavior, as we'll see.

When a "good mother" is confronted with a "badly behaving child," she can quickly get into a panic. But wasted worry about our own worth and performance all too often leads us to be shortsighted and to parent without clear intentions. Let's put our energies where they serve best—our responsibility is to guide children toward becoming cooperative, contributing members of society.

Dana has taken her three-year-old son Mark to Swiss Chalet for supper. He won't sit still for a moment. He keeps getting up and down from the table, standing on the bench seat, and invading the privacy of the couple in the next booth, as he peers over at them. When Dana tries to force him to sit still by restraining him, he screams, "Nooo!" which is worse, so she lets go and Mark is at it again, running around disturbing everyone in the restaurant.

Dana is dying of embarrassment. She wants to be strong and knows it's not good to give in to his demands, but she fears if she tries to control him again, things will escalate and the scene will worsen. Dana, like so many other "good mothers," reaches for the quick fix, either caving to his demands, bribing, or threatening him. At that moment, Dana doesn't give a hoot about effective child guidance or how Mark will be as an adult. At this point she's outraged enough she's not sure he will live to see adulthood! What she IS concerned about is not looking bad in public.

When Dana reacts to save face, what is Mark learning about mom and her authority? About himself? About others? What might he be deciding about how he should operate in the future?

MOTHERING A NEW WAY

The child guidance that I will be teaching you about in this book has long-term outcomes. I am supporting a movement back to slow parenting and balanced living. The approach is based on the influential work of personality theorist Alfred Adler. Adler's *Individual Psychology* has shaped current mainstream ideas about human behavior, growth, and development. Most forms of psychotherapy follow his basic tenets, and I think you'll agree that they make sense on an intuitive level.

Alfred Adler (1870–1937)
Alfred Adler was a physician, psychiatrist, philosopher, humanitarian, author, and educator. The applications of his ideas are found in parent education, school systems, counseling and psychotherapy, public health, mental health, business, and the arts.

The main tenets of his *Individual Psychology* are:
- *People are first and foremost social beings. They need to be connected to others in a way that gives them a feeling of belonging and acceptance. They need to contribute.*
- *People are unified and whole, with all aspects of their life being harmoniously interrelated. There is no id, ego, and superego at war within us—sorry, Freud.*
- *Ultimately, we have but three life tasks, each requiring lifelong dedication and cooperation. These are friendship, intimacy, and work.*
- *Each and every person is deserving of respect and dignity.*
- *All behavior serves a **positive** purpose. We act in ways that we believe we'll benefit from.*
- *The only way to incite change in people is to encourage them. We can only build on strengths, and everyone is strong enough.*
- *During childhood we make meaning out of our early experiences and then throughout our lives we act according to this understanding.*

Adler's humanistic approach to raising children stresses the need to take the long view. That's a tough sell when we live in a fast "Drive-thru" culture that would have us rear our children with the same speed and haste as it would have us eat our super-sized combo #4 while driving. We turn to reward charts on the fridge and administer Ritalin like gumdrops, with no view to the long-term outcomes of these tactics.

> *Ask yourself, what am 1 trying to accomplish with my parenting? When my job is finished, what do 1 hope to have achieved as my child leaves my care and enters adulthood?*

Let me compare the difference between the fast-fix parenting that helps you look good by eradicating issues immediately, and the slow parenting that encourages the development of caring, capable and cooperative young adults.

Slow Parenting	Fast-Fix Parenting
Goal: To develop responsible, cooperative and capable adults	Goal: To resolve immediate problems without consideration for long-term consequences and overall learning and development
Prepare and empower	Protect and control
Allows mistakes and sees them as opportunities to learn	Mistakes are not okay
Do with	Do for, do to

Encourages a cooperative approach to living	Encourages either rebellion and conflict or unhealthy dependency and pleasing
Win/win	Win/lose
Deals with the belief system that motivates the behavior	Deals with the behavior
Accepting	Conditional
Nonjudgmental	Judgmental
Respects differences	Insists on right and wrong, and one's own way
Parent as leader and guide	Parent as boss and nag
Allows for learning and skills to be acquired	Provides the conclusions
Uses the experience of consequences to teach and instill intrinsic motivation	Uses the experience of punishments and rewards as a form of external control
Asks: what will my children be feeling and thinking about themselves and others?	Asks: what will others be feeling and thinking about me as a parent?

Source: Adapted from resource material developed by Jody McVittie, MD, Positive Discipline Associate.

"Sign me up!" you're saying. It sure looks compelling when you see the alternatives side by side like that, doesn't it? But if you're going to adopt the slow parenting model, it requires that you make a significant reorientation of your current conceptualizations about people, and how they change, develop, and grow. Most of us have probably never even thought about these ideas consciously. But if we're to give up our "good mother" misery and get on with things the "slow way"—we must.

Good-Bye Perfection, Hello Mastery!

To adopt the "slow parenting" approach, we need to know a little something of how children grow and develop. Adler's understanding of humans and human nature is a very positivistic model. He points out that the human baby is born small and weak, clearly inferior and inadequate compared to adults. The child is, relatively speaking, in a "less than" position compared to its adult counterpart. But isn't it amazing that every healthy human baby will just naturally want to push on, mature, grow, and develop in order to overcome these inferiorities? They are naturally motivated to move toward maturation and betterment. The act of moving away from the perceived negative, or feelings of being in a "less-than state," and toward the position of perceived "plus state" is called "striving," and it's a never-ending, ongoing, lifelong process. We just keep on getting better!

The interesting thing to note here, especially in relation to misbehaviors that may later develop, is that a baby doesn't feel badly about himself because he can't yet talk or walk. Children are born with natural courage; that is, they have the courage to be imperfect humans. How hard it is to learn to walk! Children fall down over and over again. Yet, they go about the task unabashed. Why don't they just call it a day and say, "forget it, this is embarassing?" Would either you or I stick with a task that tenaciously, after so much repeated failure? What an attitude we begin life with! Young children come into this world unafraid of making mistakes. They are not afraid to show how incapable and inadequate they are to others. Why? Because children do not yet feel that inferiorities and inadequacies make them any less of a person! Let's not teach them that!

A person can either strive upwards vertically, moving "above" other people, or strive forward horizontally towards accomplishing a task. As a child, you are naturally focused on mastery. Learning to walk is simply about learning to walk. What's at stake? Only whether or not you will master the challenging motor skills necessary to pull off this unlikely evolutionary feat. But not your worth!

Let's look at both vertical and horizontal striving and see the profound ramifications a shift in direction can have for you personally, and in the way you guide your child.

Horizontal Striving
This is the orientation that "slow parenting" takes. The big point to get your head around here is that for a person to strive horizontally, she's gotta believe in the concept of "social equality." He must agree that the child who cannot yet walk or talk *is* of the same worth as a child who can.

Social equality means we believe that we are on an even plane with all fellow people, that *all* people in *any* stage of their development—and of *any* level of ability—are still equal in their worth as human beings. A child may be incapable of many things, but that doesn't mean she is worth less as a person. In fact, no one is superior or inferior to another person for *any* reason. It is a faulty notion to think of people as being better or worse than others. Nothing changes your inherent worth as person. It is firmly fixed—unflappable. Relax! Your value is secure. How wondrous! How empowering!

You not only have to philosophically agree with this, but feel it in your bones, in your whole being. Keep yourself aware of this key fact—you will be able to grow and strive positively, in a horizontal orientation.

If you can get free from the concern that your personal status might be in jeopardy (which it isn't!), you can stop worrying about failing and looking foolish and get on with concentrating on the task at hand. We really do have to be okay with ourselves right now, in our present state (whatever that may be!) before we can expect to improve. That's true for mom, but it's also true for the misbehaving child. This form of positive striving is moving toward improvement, growth, gradual self-development, and doing what needs to be done, without worry. There is no judgment here. You can be a masterful mother. Are you prepared to grow and improve as a mother? Can you accept yourself right now? Are you ready to make more mistakes? If you're not making mistakes, you're not growing. Aim for ten a day!

With horizontal striving we have a genuine care for other people's well-being (or "social interest," as Adler called it), since we are not pitted against them, jockeying for position. We work toward finding improvements to situations that achieve a mutual benefit over a self-interested benefit. Oh, it sounds so easy and even obvious—but this really is accepting the invitation to take on a lifelong challenge. I work to remind myself of these philosophical tenets every day.

Vertical Striving
Now this is a different story altogether. This is how the vast majority of people have been taught to operate in our competitive, individualistic culture. Vertical striving requires a belief in the fictional notion that people exist in a one-up/one-down fashion. Vertical striving by nature necessitates that people are part of a social pecking order, and they are therefore deemed superior or inferior to one another. In vertical thinking, those that are less capable, less mature, or less qualified are made to feel inferior. These feelings of inferiority make us terribly anxious, because we believe our personal worth and status is falling. The more inferior we feel, the more we struggle to overcome that feeling. The popular idea of the "Napoleon Complex" describes the compensatory efforts we make to overcome our feelings of inferiority with an exagger-

ated drive or by being overly ambitious. We go *way* overboard in our efforts to increase our feelings of self-worth. The smaller we feel—the bigger we act. People with superior attitudes have the greatest feelings of personal inferiority.

In vertical striving we seek superiority over others, domination over others, control over others, power over others, status over others, worth over others, and for many of us "good mothers"—we seek god-like perfection. It is competitive in nature because it views every other person as threatening since they vie for position over us too.

The table below summarizes the primary differences between vertical and horizontal striving.

Vertical Striving (Negative or Competitive Striving)	Horizontal Striving (Positive or Noncompetitive Striving)
It's all about "ME"	It's all about the *job* or *task*
How will I come out of this compared to others?	What can I contribute to help get the job done?
External motivation (praise and punishment)	Internal motivation (enjoyment and satisfaction)
Anxiety about feeling inferior	Confident and feeling like an equal
Demands perfection, mistakes are not okay	Feels courageous enough to do their best, make mistakes and learn from them

Autocratic	Democratic
Self-esteem is dependant on others' evaluation of you	Self-esteem is not in question
Creates distance between people	Creates closeness between people
Performance suffers	Performance improves
Deed = Doer	Deed = Doer
If I can't be the best, its not worth doing	If it is truly worth doing, it is worth doing regardless of how imperfectly
Perfection	Mastery

When we can accept who we are, as imperfect as we are—we gain a quality about us. It's called *being encouraged*. When we are encouraged we have the "courage" to face our imperfections and to get on with things, facing the challenges of life *despite* our inferiorities. We choose growth over retreat. We are willing to move forward, even if it means exposing our inadequacies to others. We see what needs to be done, and since we no longer need to protect our self-worth, status, or ego, we get on with growth! Now we have confidence even in a state that is imperfect. When others criticize us, we can accept it as their opinion and respect their right to have it without feeling lowered by their comments. We may even take a moment to consider the validity of their perspective, and learn from their critique!

This means that Dana can respond in the ways she feels best help deal with Mark's misbehavior in the restaurant, without having to concern herself with protecting her status or worrying about others' opinions. She can be secure in knowing her worth and value are not in jeopardy. She is free to parent effectively! You'll learn, in the chapters ahead, how to respond to dilemmas like this one and countless others. At this stage, what is most important is that Dana frees herself from the fear of others' scrutiny, so she can get on with parenting effectively.

A Seed Thought
When we plant a rose seed in the earth, we notice it is small,
but we do not criticize it as "rootless and stemless".
We treat it as a seed, giving it water and nourishment required of
a seed.

When it first shoots up out of the earth,
We do not condemn it as immature and underdeveloped;
Nor do we criticize the buds for not being open when they appear.
We stand in wonder at the process taking place and give the plant
all it needs at each stage of its development.

The rose is a rose from the time it is a seed to the time it dies.
Within it at all times, it contains its whole potential.
It seems to be constantly in the process of change;
Yet, at each stage, at each moment, it is perfectly all right as it is.
—Galloway

The Perfect Mother—Sounds Sooo Good Though
The trouble is many of us don't want to wait, grow, and develop. And no, in fact, we *don't* feel good as we are. We feel judged and we're convinced we won't be "okay" until we're perfect!

After all, the perfectionist mom is a marvel to behold. Society so reveres the person with high standards who can succeed and accomplish with ease. We LOVE that respect and recognition. She's the *übermom* with the Mary Poppins diaper bag that magically produces whatever is needed at the moment—a sterilized pacifier to replace the one that dropped in the sandbox, spare raisins to share with those "less perfect" people who forgot to pack a snack, and ipecac in case some lunatic broke into the raisin factory with a bag of wild mushrooms.

Aren't we just a *tad* envious of the feats this mom can pull off? She seems happy. She has friends, a lovely home, and great kids. She doesn't *seem* competitive—she shared the raisins, didn't she? Maybe you're not so sure you want to give this ideal up yet. But wait, before you decide, let's crack into that so-called "perfect mother brain," and see the personal cost of perfection.

The Perfect Mother's Brain—It's Strange in Here

The perfectionist epitomizes the problems that can come from being raised in the vertical, competitive childrearing model, which ties personal worth to achievements. Imagine if as a child every time you succeeded at a task your mom and dad had a veritable ticker tape parade in your honor: "Joanie made BM in the potty—get the camera [I kid you not], call Grandma, put a sticker on the potty chart." Likewise, how would it be if you were corrected for every little mistake made: "No, no—pay attention, we color *inside* the lines."

Raised in an environment of vertical striving, children are bound to come to some interesting and downright faulty conclusions about the nature of the world and of success, happiness, and human interconnectedness. These little guys are drawing conclusions about the largest questions we humans know how to ask, and they are doing it with the cognitive abilities of a preschooler. They're bound to get a few things wrong! They are also bound to feel discouraged by our misguided parenting. We are being judgmental, and even though they are being judged favorably—judgment discourages everyone.

The perfectionist's lifestyle has usually formed as a result of beliefs that are simplistic, erroneous, absolutist, and extreme. Unfortunately, these beliefs feel like truths, and they are carried right into adulthood.

The perfectionist believes:

- I must be perfect to be worthwhile; if I am not perfect I am worthless.
- A mistake means I must be a failure.
- If I make a mistake, I am less than perfect and people might reject me as a person.
- There is one definitive right way, bound by rigid rules, and if I do that I am perfect.

The other trouble with our myths or faulty beliefs is that we have a hard time breaking them, because even when we see evidence to the contrary—evidence that challenges what we believe—we discount it. So, for example, the perfectionist will tend not to see others' hard work and mistakes, though they're certainly there. Perfectionists will focus instead on great achievements or outstanding abilities, and see in others a kind of perfection they would like to emulate. They are just *so* convinced human perfection is attainable!

The Perfect Mom's Trap
With all these irrational beliefs, the perfectionist sets up a self-defeating cycle:

Mom sets an unrealistically high goal or unreasonable standard—like, say, being a perfect mother!
↓
Mom struggles with the unrelenting pressure to "be perfect."

Of course, because this goal is impossible, mom fails.

↓

Mom beats herself up about this failure with self-blame, criticism, and ridicule.

↓

This can lead to anxiety and depression as she worries about her worth.

↓

She decides that she must redouble her efforts, believing if she only tried harder, she would be perfect.

↓

Mom returns to the beginning of the cycle, this time setting an even more unrealistic and impossibly high goal.

There it is—the mad dog chasing her tail. Does the perfectionist we once idolized now seem a little less enchanting?

Thankfully, we can make the conscious decision to live a more encouraging life by choosing mastery over the superiority of perfection. We can challenge our old ideas about human worth. We can stop standing in judgment of others, ranking them as better or worse than ourselves and instead appreciate the differences between people. We can see mistakes simply as opportunities to learn. So much of our misery is self-created. Unequivocally, the first step in overcoming the feeling that we are being judged is to stop judging others. It is miraculous how a perspective change away from the good-better-best model will accomplish this. If we embrace individual differences, and see people as being in different places along their own journey of growth, it entirely alters our experience of others and of the world.

We all have our own unique myths, and we all see life through our own subjective lens. Each of us has our separate reality and opinion about everything. Come to *expect* that others have a different point of view or opinion of you as a mother.

> *"No one can make you feel inferior without your consent."*
> —Eleanor Roosevelt

MY CHILD'S MISBEHAVIOR IS MAKING ME LOOK BAD!

Okay, so you've decided to give up the ghost and move on from your perfectionist tendencies (those tendencies you decided upon when you were, say, six, and that make it so paralyzingly difficult to learn and grow through mistakes). But there you are, at the restaurant with the maroon bench seats, and your child is throwing creamers at the waitress. *Nothing* makes us feel worse about ourselves and more scrutinized than a misbehaving child. When THEY misbehave, WE are blamed. All the good intentions in the world tend to dissolve in the proverbial heat of the moment, and we revert to the repeated behavioral patterns we began to learn as children.

Well, do you *really* understand what misbehavior is all about? Do you know the role you play in it? I'd like to explain it more thoroughly from the Adlerian perspective, so you can act with clear intention and confidence, even in a situation that today may seem insurmountable.

We already discussed that the human baby comes into the world in an inferior state, and then creatively works to make sense of life, eventually creating their unique "lifestyle." That little baby is trying to figure out who he is, what others are like, and how the world operates. But of utmost importance, is the need to find a place amongst all those other people. This too is striving—striving to find one's place and a sense of belonging. The child must discover a method of behaving that creates significance and importance in relation to the others. The question is *how*.

Antonella is getting supper together when her four-year-old, Tony, comes into the kitchen. She asks Tony if he'd like to help make a salad. Tony pushes a chair up to the counter and he rips the lettuce into the salad bowl. Antonella tells Tony how much she appreciates his help.

Each experience helps Tony solve the simplistic yet powerful rubric of his lifestyle:

Life is _____
Others are: _____
I am:_____
Therefore, to cope/belong/survive in the world I must:

_____

We can't say for sure what Tony is deciding for himself about the experience, we can only hazard a guess. But Tony is probably coming up with the idea that life is a pretty happy and safe place. He is no doubt coming to see that people are kind, and that he is a likeable guy. He is also learning that by helping out he can find a way to belong. This is positive striving! He feels good about his worth and he is helping others. We're off to a good start.

Tony's next job is to wash the potatoes. He turns the water on in the sink so hard that when he puts a potato under the water, it sends water everywhere. This is a mistake, *not* a misbehavior, but depending on how mom responds, it will either fortify or reduce the probability of Tony doing this behavior again. If mom becomes agitated and busy with Tony and the cleanup, he might learn that splashing water is a way to get mom's attention and involvement. If mom can manage to stay calm without bursting a perfectionistic blood vessel over the mess just made, Tony learns that mistakes are okay and that he can manage life's little learning curves without there being any social repercussions. He continues to strive positively.

Keeton is coloring at his little table in the kitchen while mom prepares supper. He keeps taking his markers and drawing on the table instead of the paper. His mom keeps reminding him over and over again that markers belong on the paper and telling him to be careful, and to watch out. She threatens to take them away, but she never does. She watches him carefully to make sure he is drawing on the paper.

I think we'd agree that Keeton is misbehaving rather than making a mistake. His actions are purposeful. He colors off the paper for a reason. What is the purpose of this behavior?

Dr. Rudolph Dreikurs, who was Adler's protégé, believed that all children first try to find their way of belonging through cooperative means, and it is *only* when they become discouraged and can't find positive methods for belonging that they turn to the negative uncooperative methods that we call "misbehavior."

Keeton doesn't mind coloring all over the tabletop. He doesn't feel this is a problem. In fact, it's a *solution* to a problem he feels he has. Keeton has simply discovered a way to keep his mom's attention on him. He's discovered if he draws quietly he gets ignored, but if he writes on the table, mom will pay attention to him. Seems he can't get her attention by acting cooperatively, so he switches to the uncooperative method.

CHILDREN MISBEHAVE SIMPLY BECAUSE IT WORKS!
Remember that, as with perfectionism, our behaviors fall from our beliefs. Children have their myths, just like we good mothers do. To understand human behavior we HAVE to look at the beliefs behind the behavior.

Too much of the parenting advice floating around out there just slaps a bandage on the "symptom." Tell me, if you had a pain in your chest, wouldn't you need to know if it's heartburn or a heart attack before you decided on your treatment plan? It's imperative that we understand the root of the child's misbehavior before we decide on a plan of action for correction and guidance. I want to help you learn to "diagnose" the goal of your children's misbehavior. Let's find out what they are trying to accomplish, and then guide them toward the positive, cooperative method of attainment.

Children have only four goals they try to reach through mistaken means (a.k.a. misbehavior):

1. Attention
2. Power
3. Revenge
4. Avoidance

It is important to understand the difference between these four goals, because our parenting strategies will be different for each one. For example, if a child is attempting to gain power, you won't solve the dilemma by giving her attention. Lets look at each of these four goals separately in order to understand children's beliefs, and how our reactions are making these methods "work" for them.

Attention
The attention-seeking child has the erroneous belief that he is only important when people are paying attention to him. If people *don't* pay attention, he feels he must no longer be important. We know that this is not true. But children don't. They act in accordance with their beliefs, and they figure out any way they can to keep themselves in the spotlight and to keep you paying attention and engaged with them. Usually, that's through disturbances, like splashing water or plucking leaves off the houseplants. Sometimes it's from pulling you into their service by making you carry them, or spoonfeed them, or sit up all night with them while they do their homework.

How do we know the goal is attention? We usually feel very annoyed and frustrated; we spend a lot of time "dealing" with attention-seeking children. We nag them, remind them, and often we just do what needs to be done *for* them. However we respond, we need to understand that it is *that* response, that kneejerk reaction that's providing the payoff that makes their behavior work for them. We don't "cause" our children to misbehave, but we do make it beneficial to them by the way we respond.

The trick for mom is to recognize that the behavior is for the sole purpose of gaining her attention. If mom can catch that idea, then she can ignore the behavior so that the child learns experientially that his old tricks are no longer effective. Mom can pop Keeton's crayons away without any words or malice. The child will abandon a behavior that is not working. Of course, we are not done our parenting job yet—we still have the belief to deal with. We still have to work to encourage children about their worth, and show them positive ways to connect with us when they are *not* demanding it.

Power

Power is also critical for our children to have. Don't get down on the word "power." We want our children to feel empowered. However, if they can't find empowerment through feeling competent and by having some say and control in their lives, then sure enough, they will seek it out through negative means, often by finding strength in looking big and bossy. The more you rob a child of power, the more the child comes off bullying you, just like ole Napoleon.

We can determine if power is the child's goal by noticing how we are feeling. Attention was annoying—but, oh man, now we're MAD. We respond to power-seeking children by fighting, and we fight to win! Needless to say, things escalate.

We need to find ways for children to experience positive power in the family. They are telling us through their behavior that they need to feel empowered, that currently they feel disempowered. They're letting us know they're ready for more control over their lives. We're scared to give our children power, thinking they'll give us more grief—but it's actually the opposite. If they have positive power, they don't need to find negative power. In the chapters ahead, I'll show you how. Seems Mark needs to find some way to feel powerful other than showing his mom he can defeat her with his restaurant antics.

Revenge

No, you don't have a violent sociopath on your hands. Moms with children who have revenge as a goal are usually very discouraged by family life. Things have become bad for everyone. Children never seek revenge first. It's always in response to a hurt they perceive that they have been dealt. They want to "get even." The goal of revenge is to show parents that they won't be discounted by us and the way we treat them. They aim to show us how hurt they feel. Let's take that message to heart. The children with the worst behaviors are also the children carrying the most pain. Moms have to deal with the hurt and pain. Learn to listen to your children. LISTEN so you can hear how they feel. LISTEN so you can try to step inside their subjective reality and see life through their lens. Why does it feel so hurtful to them? Too often we discount their feelings as being "wrong," as in "I do *not* love the baby more than you—you're WRONG—now smarten up."

Avoidance

This is the last of the four goals and it represents the deepest level of discouragement children can feel. They have come to believe that they can't belong. That is a very sad feeling. It is their belief that no effort will bring success, and they give up. The child's worth is nearly bankrupt, and she can't manage any more failure. So, she figures if you don't try you can't lose, right? Children feign such convincing helplessness that as parents we end up throwing our hands in the air as if to say, "I give up. I have tried everything with this kid!" Of course, that is what they hope to accomplish! It really takes the pressure off if no one expects anything of you.

As moms who now understand the goal-directed nature of misbe-havior, we must make sure our children don't feel we have given up on them, ever. We have to recognize through their behavior that they believe us to be a pressure on them. Our job is back off on the pressure, while showing faith in our children. They need to know they are loved and valuable just the way they are now. When they restore their feeling of being worthwhile and okay as they are, they can begin to grow again!

I am providing you with a summary chart below so you can practice doing your own goal "diagnosing."

THE FOUR GOALS OF MISBEHAVIOR

Child's Myth or Faulty Belief	Child's Goal	Clue #1: Parent Feels	Clue #2: Parents' Typical Fast-Fix Reaction in the Moment	Clue #3: Child's Reaction to the Correction	Slow Parenting (Choices for Alternate Responses)
I belong and am significant only when I am being noticed or served.	Attention	Annoyed.	Remind Coax Do for…	Stops temporarily only to resume again later or disturb in another way.	Ignore the behavior (not the child). Give positive attention when it is not being demanded. Avoid giving special service. STOP giving payoff with your talking and get into ACTION.
I belong and am significant only when I am the boss, or when I am proving that no one is the boss of me!	Power	Angry Provoked, feeling their authority is being threatened	Fight Give in	Fights back and things get worse. Or Child succumbs to your authority with defiant compliance.	Refuse to fight. Disengage from the conflict. Show the child constructive forms of power by increasing their skills and capabilities. Realize that both fighting and giving in serve to stimulate children's desire for power.

Belief	Goal	Feeling	Reaction	Child's Response	What To Do
I can feel my significance by hurting others, as I feel hurt by them. I cannot be loved.	Revenge	Hurt	Retaliate / Get even	Retaliates with same or new weapon.	Heal the hurting. Time for lots of open dialogue and communication. Learn to LISTEN.
I can't belong, so it is no use trying. I must convince people not to expect anything from me. I am helpless and unable.	Avoidance	Despair / "I give up"	Giving up / Overhelping	Retreats further. Shows no improvement.	Don't give up on them! Notice improvement and effort. ENCOURAGE ENCOURAGE ENCOURAGE!

In every case of misbehavior, we must remember that we have a child who is simply discouraged about his worth and belonging. If we can help him find a way out of his discouragement, help him find a way to feel a sense of belonging through useful means of contributing and participating gainfully in family life—misbehavior will cease. Children, like adults, will strive in a positive way if they are unencumbered by feelings of inadequacy. Mom can help by learning to be encouraging, and by recognizing that her reactions and responses are actually sustaining the misbehavior. The coming chapters will show you in detail how some of these misbehaviors play out within the family dynamic, and how our "good mom myths" continue to get in the way of providing the encouragement our children truly need.

But before we get down to the serious myth-busting, there's one other all-important area of family life that must be explored. Yup, next we'll bash the myth "my marriage can wait." Even if you're blissfully happy and co-parenting with ease—there are still nuggets of information that you will be oh-so-glad to pick up!

CHAPTER 3

MYTH:
MY MARRIAGE CAN WAIT

L et me ask you straight up: How is your marriage? Have you even thought about it recently? Most of us are too busy switching up loads of laundry and organizing the car pool to give this question serious consideration. Too often we slide down a slippery slope, oblivious to just how far we've let things go, until one day we wake up and feel we are lying in bed next to a stranger.

The commonly held belief of our generation is that all the family energies should go to the children. I would like to challenge that myth. Good mothers who put their children first, subordinate the importance of their marriage. We seem to believe that our marriages are made of titanium and are able to withstand the neglect and abuses that can sometimes come with starting a family. Who doesn't want to think that their marriage is strong and stable, capable of withstanding the added pressures of beginning a family? It's a contract after all—"'til death do us part." Our children, on the other hand, will only be young and needy for this short time, or so we tell ourselves. We think that as mature, patient adults, the needs of the coupleship can be shelved. After all, we have signed on to be there through sickness and health, richer and poorer, so surely we can hang in through the tribulations of starting a family.

But the divorce rate tells us otherwise. Almost half of all children will have divorced parents, and only 25 percent of remarriages survive. Helping our marriages to be healthy and strong *does* help our children, but it takes effort. When we moms focus solely on our children, down to their tiniest needs, and leave our relationship with our spouses to go fallow, it's as if we're straightening the deck chairs on the Titanic! We're paying so much attention to the little niggly details (how will I find the ideal summer camp, and where did I put that yellow-spotted sock?), we forget to see the whole big picture: We fail to notice that we're actually tanking!

> *Couples that come for counseling report that they have been unhappy for an average of six years. That's too much of your life to waste in misery, and your marriage is too important!*

In this chapter our marriages are going to be in the spotlight so we can poke some holes in that old myth that our marriages can wait. We'll look at the stages of marriage, the transition to a family, and the many different ways your relationship with your partner impacts your children. We'll discuss a few of the biggy challenges that people face as they move from being a couple to becoming a family—division of labor, different parenting styles, and yes siree, we'll talk about sex stresses, too!

I have never known a marriage to fail if the couple wanted to make it work—no matter what had happened in the past. Let's make sure yours doesn't fail either.

STAGES OF MARRIAGE

Experts agree that marriage is actually an evolutionary process that goes through several distinct stages. I think it's helpful for couples to know that their marriage changes in important ways. Let's look at them.

Stage 1: Romance/Honeymoon

The name says it all, really. We are in love and there is nothing that's gonna get in our way! We have left the safety of the love we found in our families growing up, moved through the nervous time of exploring our new independence in the big world, and now we have intertwined our heart with a soul mate. Often this stage is referred to as *limerence*, or "being in love," which is distinct from simply "loving" someone. In limerence we are walking on air! We love how we feel about our partner, and we adore how they make us feel. It's a euphoric time and we just can't seem to get enough of each other. Needless to say, the sexual expression of that love makes it a dynamic time in the bedroom for both parties, too.

But limerence, lovely as it feels, is a time-limited event—it lasts about five years for most couples. Many people confuse the passing out of the limerence phase with "falling out of love," and this confusion results in a high number of affairs and divorces for couples at this time. They feel it must be over since they don't feel that "special love" with their partner anymore. Sure the highs are not as high and the lows also aren't as low, but in reality that means the coupleship is actually moving towards more stability. The predictability and dependability may seem boring compared to the excitement of limerence, but it means there's a great strength developing in the relationship.

Stage 2: Reality Stage

This stage happens for most couples between the ages of 25 and 50. We spend a long time in this phase and it is characterized by the infiltration of life's realities into our little love and lust bubble. We are forced to face situations as a couple that may make us think twice about our partners and the pre-existing assumptions we had about them. Now we have to squeeze in our moment of loving between the demands of a career, housework, caring for aging parents, and raising young kids. This phase of marriage can be a vulnerable time. Women who felt adored and wanted in their early marriage may now feel taken for granted and rejected. Likewise, men who once felt they were looked up to and respected, often feel belittled and less important. However, we really can keep fun and intimacy alive in a marriage if we make a point to carve out time for it. This stage of a relationship is pivotal: we can deepen our bond and enjoy the fruits of overcoming obstacles together, or we can drive each other away. Don't worry—reality can be a surprisingly wonderful place to have a relationship! We can learn to more deeply communicate and better deal with interpersonal issues, especially if we seek out support when we need to through counseling or coaching.

Stage 3: Stuck and Hurting

We know that the realities of Stage 2 will create some conflict, and that both partners will experience hurts and disappointments. How these conflicts resolve is critical to the health of the relationship. Hurts left unresolved fester and grow into bitterness, hatred, and a cold distance that drives the couple apart. In this phase, couples stop relating in their relationship and really become nothing more than unhappy roommates harboring ill will for each other. This stage is characterized by feelings of claustrophobia and hopelessness, and the sense that it would be impossible to bring about changes in the marital patterns. Don't despair if you feel you are in Stage 3! One of the great surprises in life is the resiliency of humans. Marriage counseling can help couples deal with the raw exposed nerves on the surface, or dig through the tough skin that has developed, and find that original loving heart. Forgiveness for transgressions is possible; hurts can heal. Couples can rebound with the skills learned in counseling. And in letting the ugly stuff hang out, we feel more certain we can be ourselves, more open and honest. Also, when couples successfully emerge from this stage, they feel they are closer than they would have been had they never been through such hard times.

Stage 4: Marital Maturity

When we hit our 50s, if we have managed to take care of our marriage, we hit a marital maturity that proves beautifully enriching. The sexual expression of that mature love often translates into the most gratifying lovemaking of our lives, and (it's true!) it continues into our 60s and beyond. As they leave the career and parenting push behind, couples often enter a surprisingly graceful period in their relationship; having weathered innumerable storms and survived together, this stage of the relationship can be downright golden, meaningful, and characterized by a quiet and profound gratitude for one another.

If you're reading this book on motherhood, you have likely left the bliss of Stage 1 and are entering into the challenges that face couples in Stage 2. We expect this, and starting a family is for sure one of the biggest there is! How you face these challenges determines whether you get to grow closer together, into the deep, deep connection of the later stages, or walk down the path of hurt and resentment. It is important that YOU decide this. It's not a fate thrust upon you—it's a choice you actively make and pursue as a goal. Set the goal of a happy marriage not just for yourself but also for your children. I'll give you tips on how to get started. Let's now look at how family life is a marital challenge.

TRANSITIONING FROM A COUPLE TO A FAMILY: THE CHILDREN COME FIRST

The parenting literature seems devoid of any information on this most important life transition. We can so easily get wrapped up in mothering, both the demands and pleasures of it, that we lose touch with the other roles we have in life. Children have been given such high value in our modern society that the new baby becomes the exalted one around whom all other activities must be organized. Our husbands and marriages are all too often marginalized in this process. Even Megan and Brian, who had been married for seven years and who felt their solid relationship could only grow from starting a family, felt the effects:

> Brian was so excited about becoming a dad. He often cuddled with Meg's belly, singing to his baby. He rubbed her swollen feet at the end of a long day and thought his wife

had never looked more beautiful. They took prenatal classes and Brian attended the birth, lovingly offering up ice chips for Meg to suck on and rubbing her hands. Eight hours and an epidural later, 8-lb, 7-oz BJ (Brian Junior) was born. It was a love feast of unprecedented proportions. Yet only a few months later, Brian could hardly recall feeling that way. It seemed that Megan and BJ had fallen deeply in love. She was content to give all her time and attention to BJ, so that when Brian arrived home after work and tried to cuddle with Megan or talk about his day, he was met with exhaustion and lack of interest. It had only been a short while, but already Brian felt hurt. He felt pushed out of his wife's life since the baby arrived. Instead of the baby bringing them closer, Brian felt abandoned—more like it had become two against one. Instead of bringing them closer, the baby had become a wedge between them.

Brian is an integral part of the family, and he has needs for inclusion and love that must not be subverted by the baby. He needs to feel valued rather than feeling marginalized. Adult or child, we can't have "outliers" in our families.

I suppose the positive of Megan and Brian's case is that the baby will benefit from being incredibly well loved and cared for, right? Wrong!

OUR CHILDREN DON'T COME "FIRST?"

We have bought in to the societal notion of the child's importance and we live by the doctrine that "our children come first." I would like to present an alternate myth.

I believe children *join* a family. In order for children to achieve a sense of belonging, they need to feel "a part of" the family, not *above* the others, nor *below* them. It is in being equal, and through participation and contribution that we feel connected and a part of our families. Everyone participates in the give and take of family life—even the baby. We all work to meet *everyone's* needs.

"If Only I Knew Then …"

If you've got your eyes focused entirely on the tiny swaddled creature sleeping in the crib while your beautiful and frustrated partner is doing a handstand in the living room trying to win back even five minutes of your attention, it may be time to learn a lesson from moms who have been there, done that.

In larger families, a new baby arrives in a world already populated with older siblings who also have needs. These infants learn from their earliest experiences that they must share mom's time. After all, if she's busy getting one toddler into a snowsuit while another sibling is asking for help getting his zipper started, the hungry baby in the basinet waits until mom is available. She can't drop everything and begin to nurse. The baby is "made" to wait because of the simple reality of the situation, and thus learns to be a team player! Mom is not being negligent. The situation demands that the baby wait for a couple of minutes, and lo and behold, the baby learns to wait! The baby learns early cooperation!

Cynthia's third child would sit contented in her bouncy chair on the kitchen table amusing herself by watching her siblings' commotion and looking at the sunlight dance in patterns on the ceiling. Cynthia had terrible guilt that this child got less of her time and attention than her first two children. As time unfolded and her children grew, Cynthia came to see that her youngest child was very easy-going and cooperative, while her first-born (whom she doted on and who was excused from the need to be cooperative because mom would jump at his every wish) continued to be a more demanding and less cooperative child. "If only I had known this when I had my first, I would have backed off far more."

Yes, a newborn is taxing, but that only further supports the notion that we must bear the load *with our partner*. We also have to feel appreciated for our efforts: we need to feel valued for what we are doing for the family. Mommies and daddies need to figure out how to do this *with* and *for* each other. We need to create families that are a place to find love, acceptance, encouragement, importance, and belonging—not only for our children, but for ourselves! Our families are our wellsprings, and for the parents, that largely comes from each other and the health of the marriage.

Moms and dads need to remember that beyond their co-parenting responsibilities they are also friends and lovers. If taking time for your coupleship feels like it's taking away from the kids, think of it as actually benefiting your children, as it will keep the team strong and together. Besides, what other investment has the potential to pay you back in dividends like full emotional support, back rubs, and lots of belly laughs? And hey, this investment continues to compound over a lifetime. Nice returns!

NIP IT IN THE PROVERBIAL "BUD"

During "Stage 2," when your marriage is volatile from the strains of starting a family and navigating careers, make sure you invest in the long-term health of your marriage through the simple gestures that keep the coupleship in your forethoughts. Don't feel guilty taking time or money from the children. Believe me, they will thank you for being loving happy parents!

- Take a moment every day to be affectionate (hug, kiss, snuggle, spoon in bed …).
- Take five minutes every day to catch up on how the other person's day went—it will go a long way in keeping you connected.
- Take one day a week and date! Claim this special no-kid time just for each other. It doesn't need to be big

event. The key is frequency! Share some wine and cheese and watch a movie together. Step out for breakfast one morning, or rendezvous for lunch.

- Take one week a year as a romantic couple's holiday. If you're feeling like you don't want to be romantic and can't imagine you'd have fun for a week alone with your husband, book two weeks—you're in trouble already!

When was the last time you dropped the baby off at your mother's and went on a date with your partner? When was the last time you kissed your way through a movie, or gave each other a foot rub, or took a bath together? These simple beautiful moments are a huge part of how we communicate our love for one another, and yet they are most often the first things to go out the window when the baby arrives. Take time for love!

HOW MARRIAGES IMPACT CHILD DEVELOPMENT

Your marriage itself is actually influencing your child's development. Let me share with you how that works:

> *Your relationship serves as the children's big "guide book" to how humans get along. Being emotionally healthy yourself and being in loving and respectful relationships is the **best** environment to create for your children—bar none. Everything and anything else can be endured if your children have this piece in place!*

Alfred Adler believed that all child guidance is about helping prepare our children to face the three major challenges of social living, or "how to survive life in a herd," as I like to say. He called these challenges the Three Life Tasks: Love, Friendship, and Work. In this trio, your marriage represents the love task. How you handle your own marriage is partially a result of your own childhood training, and now *your* relationship is acting as a powerful educational documentary that your own children are watching and learning from. In children's formative years, it is mom and dad's relationship that provides the information about how adult humans are supposed to do this thing called "getting along" or "cooperating."

*If you want your children to be loving, caring, and cooperative, **let them see you being** loving, caring, and cooperative with your partner.*

"I couldn't understand why Natalie, my five-year-old, would always sulk when she didn't get her way. It really irritated me. Then one day I caught myself being quiet and down after my husband had told me that we couldn't afford to put in the new swing set I wanted for the kids. I realized that I was sulking! She had learned this tactic from watching me try to get my way with my husband. I decided from that moment on that I would find better ways to deal with such issues with my husband, just as I wanted Natalie to handle things better with me."

—Linda, mother of Natalie, 5, and Aaron, 3

"I remember yelling at my husband about how he had treated our son. I said, 'Don't talk to him like that!' Then I realized that I was yelling at my husband just as much as he was yelling at my son. What was the good of that? Clearly, we were a yelling household, and he was just picking up and adapting to the family culture we had created."

—Sally, mother of Tess, 10, Ben, 6, and Emma, 2

DON'T PANIC: A GOOD MARRIAGE IS NOT NECESSARILY CONFLICT-FREE

If you take *any* two humans and put them together, after a while, I promise you they will need to deal with some kind of conflict. Conflict isn't the issue. It's *how* we deal with inevitable conflict that's important. After all, that is the essence of "cooperating," isn't it? How will we cooperate and function together, given our inherent differences?

Open respectful discourse that ends in a resolution all parties can accept, even if it's simply to agree to disagree, is healthy. Kids see that mom and dad get angry with one another, but most importantly, that they still love each other and they resolve their issues. That is effective parenting. This doesn't mean I invite you to have a hissy fit and scream at your partner over his upset at the $100 night cream you just bought. But for all those good mothers out there who just went pale at the thought of the damage they inflicted during last night's angry spat: RELAX! This is not yet another example of something you now have to strive to do perfectly. Modeling great relationship skills means living in reality: arguments happen, people become frustrated and angry, and not every situation is handled perfectly. But when you start from the base of loving, respecting, and caring for your partner, you are teaching your children not only the reality that nothing is perfect, but also how to resolve tough issues.

Trish and Darren had an argument about spending money on a large house expense. The disagreement was about whether repairing the broken pool was discretionary spending or essential. They were both passionate about their polarized points of view on this matter. Trish could feel herself ramping up to explode in response to the feeling that she was losing the argument. In the end, they hugged and apologized for letting things get out of hand, and decided they could solve this better if they weren't fighting about it. They both wanted the same thing, they just needed to find a good path to get there. They managed to move it out of the personal and into problem solving. Their children were okay with the short explosion when they saw that their parents had been able to calm down and were now working toward a win/win resolution.

THESE FIGHTS KEEP GETTING LONGER AND LONGER

Too many people get blindsided waiting to seek help or enrichment. You would take your car in for a checkup if it felt like the motor wasn't running on all its cylinders or if you heard a strange and terrible knocking! Do you wait for your car to completely break down before seeing the mechanic? No—you check it out and get it back to running smoothly. I suggest you do the same with your marriage. Have high standards! Demand to be happy and content!

If you're reluctant to consider counseling, do any of these excuses sound familiar?

- I don't have time.
- I don't have the energy to tackle those problems with everything else going on.
- I am afraid that if I start talking about that pink elephant in my living room, things will get worse instead of better.
- My partner won't go.
- My friend went and said it didn't really do anything.
- It's expensive.
- Things aren't great, but they don't seem *that* bad.
- I can do this on my own—I just have to try harder.
- He needs personal therapy—it's not my issue.

- The situation is already beyond repair.
- I don't want to hear about the stuff I already know I am not doing well.

Now reread the list of excuses and ask yourself if any of these obstacles is so great that you would sacrifice your marriage for it. You may feel like you don't have the time or the money for counseling, but believe me, the hours and the money you could spend with divorce lawyers is far, far more.

Let's look at some of the more common issues that crop up, especially in the early years of starting a family, and apply some counseling techniques right now.

Common phrases heard from children raised in families with healthy marriages:

- *"Yuck—take it somewhere else, you two lovebirds!" (Show your affection.)*
- *"Will you show me what you and Mommy are learning at your salsa classes?" (Find interests to do together—besides parenting.)*
- *"Gramma says she can't wait to spoil us all weekend long while you guys are off on your weekend away." (Take time away—for just the two of you—to be a couple again.)*
- *"Wow, I thought Mom was going to be so scared to tell Dad about dinting the car, but she wasn't. Maybe I can tell him about losing my expensive baseball glove after all. (Model to your children how to handle life, problems, and conflict.)*

THE MOTHER BEEF: IS HE LAZY, OR DISCOURAGED?

The biggest complaint I get about dads is that they don't pull their parenting weight. However, moms who wear the "good mother" title can inadvertently discourage their husbands and push them out of their rightful parenting role. One such mom complained that she hadn't a moment to herself since the baby was born because she could not leave her baby with her husband. "Why?" I asked? She replied, "Because he's useless." I asked her what her husband did for a living, seeing as he was so "useless." Turns out he was a marketing executive. I had to challenge her estimation of his abilities: "He clearly has some brains about him—I'll bet he is probably resourceful enough to make it through an afternoon alone with his one-year-old daughter."

I went on to challenge her to see the difference between "can't" and "won't" or being simply unwilling. She was not worried that harm would befall them, but rather that things would not be done *her* way, or that they would have to struggle together. Sure, maybe her daughter would cry. Hell, maybe her husband would come to tears, but look at the cost of this decision. By *not* leaving her husband with his daughter, she was demeaning both of them because, in essence, she sends the discouraging message: I don't trust you two to manage together the way I think you should.

Mom's protection of them denies them the chance to build important, needed skills and to have a relationship together.

We are all neophytes with our first babies. We have to learn how to bathe a slippery creature that seemingly has no bones, and master diaper changes, even those impressive ones of yellow poop that's managed to travel all the way up to the collar of the sleeper. Yes, we all learn to do this the same way, not from reading a "how to" book, but simply by doing it, time and time again. We gain competence through practice. We learn the sounds of different cries, and the preferred games, and how to recognize when they are tired or hungry.

The reality is, fathers' ability to gain these skills is usually impacted by our society's arrangement that they typically are the secondary caregiver (at least initially). Even by the time you're discharged from the hospital, mom has put in far more hours of listening to crying and trying to figure out how to soothe the baby than dad has. The gap between your abilities can continue to grow. That is not important. What is critical is how moms respond and react to this disparity. Do you act in ways that encourage dad to stay involved and gain his own competencies, or do you inadvertently discourage him into avoidance and sometimes into giving up completely?

John loved his Saturday mornings with Emily. His work schedule was tough and he was often home only after she was already in bed. The weekends were important father–daughter time for him. One such Saturday John took the initiative to take Emily to the park, but just as he was packing up to leave, Elaine started with a litany of what she felt were helpful instructions. Her help was perceived as criticism, and a display of her general distrust for his ability. It was death by a thousand paper cuts.

"Did you remember the sun block? Including the tops of her ears?"

"How much did she eat this morning? Did you even *try* to get her to eat?"

"Take this other jacket—that one is too light for this weather."

"Don't let her fall asleep on the way home or she'll never go down for her afternoon nap."

"This time—when you go to the park, play with her. Don't just sit and read the paper."

It's times like these that it's good to remember what it's like to be a new learner. If your supervisor had come over to your computer and just smacked away at a keyboard to fix a problem you were having, would you have learned? When we take over and are overly critical, or when we blather on with advice, we do nothing to further the learning process. Step back, take a breath, and have faith! Dad can manage any crisis that might arise.

One of the more creative ways I have seen for encouraging dads around their parenting is to create a parenting group for your circle of friends. Here's how one group set themselves up:

- Families meet every Sunday from 5 to 8 p.m.
- All the families pitch in to hire a couple of teenage babysitters for the children.
- Kids get playtime, pizza, and a movie.
- Parents take their pizza to the basement, and fill a cooler with ice for the BYO beer to be chilled.
- The group works like any book club, with each family purchasing and reading though the same parenting book and discussing it chapter by chapter.
- Certain couples are given a chapter or two to quickly review, so those who don't get the reading done are up to speed.

Discuss, compare thoughts, share stories, and build a community of support! You don't need an expert—just a good book.

WHAT TO DO WHEN YOU AND YOUR PARTNER PARENT DIFFERENTLY

Jeff was such a tender and loving fiancé and husband, but Charlotte was shocked to see that with children he ruled with an iron fist. This was *not* the Jeff she would have expected, and she certainly didn't agree with his autocratic style. Charlotte was not going to let her husband deal with the kids in that

way! Often after dad came down on the children and made
them cry, it ended in Charlotte yelling at Jeff, and then crying herself. Why wouldn't he listen to her ideas about how
to handle discipline? Charlotte was appalled that Jeff could
treat people that disrespectfully. She hated him for making her children cry! Charlotte actually pitied her children
for having him as a father and tried to make it up to them.
Even though Jeff treated Charlotte the same as before they
had children, Charlotte wondered if she could love such a
seemingly cold brute.

Another big source of marital stress that comes part and parcel
with starting a family is the issue of conflicting parenting styles.
Moms and dads hear that it's important to be on the same page
and to present a united front to the children. They're hoping to
be consistent. Of course, that would be lovely and a nice ideal,
but no matter how philosophically aligned you are, there will be
differences in how you deal with discipline. These differences can
become a huge source of marital conflict—as with Charlotte and
Jeff—but they don't have to.

You Are One of Two Parents
Let me set the record straight on parents with different parenting
ideas and styles. While you all make up one family, each of you will
have your own independent relationships with each of your children. Healthy relationships exist when you don't fall into the trap
of triangulating issues and interfering in other people's matters. The
big principle here is to mind your own business and let people own
their relationships. When we step in and try to improve, correct,
or compensate for other people's relationships, we create havoc.
Children quickly learn that things are different with mom and with
dad. We don't need to pity them—they can handle themselves with
dad. In fact, when children see mom upset with dad over his disci-

pline, they learn to stir the pot on purpose in order to keep mom's concern and acts of loving compensation coming!

> *"Ben, my husband, is a pushover. He can't stand to see his little girl cry. Whenever it's his night to do tuck-ins, she wails when he leaves and he gets roped into her tears, gives way to her demands, and ends up lying with her until she falls asleep. I've told him that he's teaching her the wrong thing by giving in to her tears, but he just won't listen to me. His caving undermines all the work I've done to be strong on this point. Grrr! It infuriates me."*
>
> *—Sandra, mother of Abigail (3)*

When I spoke with this mom, she confirmed what I suspected: her daughter doesn't cry when she does the tuck-in. The daughter knows it will be of no use with mom, because she doesn't give the payoff that her daughter is looking for. This difference doesn't confuse the child at all. Far more problematic would be individual inconsistencies, such as would occur if dad sometimes caved in and lay down with her, and at other times blew up at her for crying. *That* would make life feel scary and unpredictable to the child.

Here are two simple agreements that partners with different parenting styles can make with one another:

1. *Whoever starts the discipline has to finish it.* Don't undermine each other's efforts by stepping in. If dad got upset and turned off the TV, let dad deal with the rest of the fallout too. If your children appeal to you for help, claiming, "that's no fair—dad turned off the TV, you never do that!" you can simply state, "I am sorry you are having

trouble with your dad—I am sure you two will figure it out. This is between the two of you." Then, afterwards, if you want to discuss with your partner how a situation was handled, you can do so. But if after you discuss it you can only agree to disagree, that is fine.

2. *Don't compensate for the other's supposed deficiencies.* When you try to make up for what you perceive to be your partner's shortcomings (perhaps by buying extra things for the children or spoiling them with later bedtimes, etc), you are actually confirming or informing the children that they *should* feel put out by their other parent's treatment.

BEDROOM INTIMACY REFLECTS RELATIONSHIP HEALTH

Lovemaking is the ultimate in trust, closeness, and cooperation. If you're silently at war with one another, you probably don't want to sleep with the enemy! The whole essence of your relationship is played out under the sheets.

So, how is your sex life?

Quiz
___ You're so sleep-deprived that you don't understand the question.

___ Your husband invites you to have sex in the living room because your bed is full of children.

___ You know exactly the last time you had sex, not because it was last night, but because it was the day you conceived your third child, who is now entering nursery school.

___ You're thinking to yourself, "Sex? That would involve us both being in the same bed at the same time, wouldn't it?"

___ You've convinced yourself that once you get your pre-pregnancy figure back, maybe your defunct libido will come with it.

___ You don't even want to talk to him right now, let alone sleep with him!

If you checked off any of these items, it's time to take a close look at what's going on at a deeper level in your marriage. Let's "look under the hood" and see if we need to get into counseling for some roadside assistance.

Don't get me wrong—we all understand that your love life takes a hit when you first have kids. You're physically tired, your breasts are doing double duty as a milk factory, and your body is still recuperating from childbirth. But these reasons can also act as excuses to avoid it.

> Rick and Darlene had not shared a bed in two years. They had three kids who were all poor sleepers, so somehow the family ritual just ended up being easier on everyone if mom slept with Toby (3) and dad slept with Sarah (5).

I can sure empathize with how tiring having three children under five is. I'm sure that when tuck-ins are happening, the adults are probably just as zonked as the kids. But when I hear of families where the parents have abandoned the matrimonial bed, I have to probe to see if this is a yellow flag for Stage 2 distress that's going unchecked, hidden behind the myth that sex and intimacy are supposed to be sacrificed in the name of having little kids. Couples operating under this myth are experiencing a growing distance in their intimacy, and chalking it up to "normal" and "expected." Sure it's nice to cuddle with your children—but not to the exclusion of cuddling with your partner! Moms and dads need to get back into bed together, and they need to resume their sexual life.

There is no right amount of sex to be having, so long as both partners feel satisfied. But letting your love life go means you miss the restorative element of lovemaking that reconnects you as a couple.

Many "good mothers" don't feel sexual at all. Sometimes we wear that virginal mother crown so tightly that we can't take it off and get our mind around being a lover again. There actually is a quick fix for this: it's called "fake it 'til you make it." Why? Because sometimes women need to actually engage in sexual foreplay and intercourse in order to get aroused and to re-create a desire. How can we do that if we keep refusing to start? Be willing to try. Commence sexual play when you are NOT in the mood, and see if the tides turn. If you wait 'til you feel amorous, you could wait so long that you never get your engines revving together again!

PARENTAL SEX TIPS

- Get a hotel room for a night. (Note: Does getting a hotel room for the night sound like a cliché? Something becomes a cliché when it's repeated *so often* it becomes boring and loses its original intensity and meaningfulness. I defy you to make booking a hotel room for just the two of you a cliché!)
- Sneak home for a quickie while the kids are out
- Make a date of it, and then look forward to it *all* day.
- Buy a lock for your bedroom door if you're worried about little intruders (hide the key in your sexiest underwear).
- Buy new undergarments that are sexy instead of functional.
- Go to bed *before* you're dog-tired.
- Fake it 'til you make it—give yourself permission to start cold and then warm to the idea.

If the idea of sex is still not interesting to you, see your physician or a marriage counselor and find out what's up. There could be more to the story. Sexual intimacy helps our marriages, so honor it as a priority and attend to this part of your coupleship. Don't drop your expectations and abandon your love life, especially not "for your children's sake." When you're happy and content—they're happy and content. You'll parent better if you have a little bounce in your step!

As a family and marriage therapist, I feel passionate about eradicating misinformation and helping people understand some important concepts that are very easy to implement once they've been shared. I want to give "good mothers" permission to find a babysitter and stake some claim in their partner, the marriage, and their love life. Your marriage cannot sustain an 18-year hiatus while you raise kids, and a vibrant marriage will help you enjoy your children more.

CHAPTER 4

MYTH:
GOOD MOTHERS ARE ALL-CARING AND ALL-PROTECTING

GOOD MOTHERS ARE ALL-CARING AND ALL-PROTECTING

You turn your back for just one teeny tiny little second and boom! He's gone like a shot—out of your sight. Where's my toddler? Eating the ibuprofen "candy" he discovered in my purse? Choking on the one stray marble that rolled away unnoticed from his sister's Kerplunk game? Or, has he brilliantly managed to find the only patch of lead paint left on a windowsill in North America and is contentedly sucking on it? These are the tiring years of hypervigilance.

You work so hard to keep their little bodies from harm's way and you still have all the emotional and psychological concerns to fret about. Will they overcome their separation anxiety? Are they "securely attached?" Are they being bullied by that brat Tyler at daycare? What to do? God forbid we do the wrong thing and the kid ends up in the hospital or psychologically damaged. You pray, "Please, no! Don't let me screw them up the way my childhood did me!"

There just always seems to be something! Sure they grow up, but then you worry about the other stuff you read about in the paper: youth gangs, STDs, and "Robotripping." You're perplexed by all you hear about teenagers and safety, especially given their cyber life on these new "social networks" (or whatever the heck they are). Dr. Spock didn't write a chapter on *that*, did he?

We love and care for our children so very deeply that we'll go to any lengths to protect them. But, I swear, at every turn we're told of another thing we're supposed to be concerned about. Have you noticed that the list just keeps growing? We're trying to keep up with all the news because if anything ever happened to our children and we thought we might have been able to avoid it, well, we just couldn't live with ourselves. We're left with a feeling that life is a really harsh place for children, and we're told they're so vulnerable and fragile that mothers must make sure their children are protected.

We do have the obligation to protect our children from harm, no

question there. But what of dints and bruises? Stress and strains—
both physical and mental? Where do you draw the line? Better safe
than sorry seems to be the policy, so we cover them in bubble wrap
and hermetically seal them off from the world.

This overprotection of children is called "pampering," and it can
be more damaging to their development than neglect or abuse. Yet,
our current, unchallenged good-mothering culture is based on a
pampering style, without anyone having any idea whatsoever that
their actions are harmful. We are simply living by the standard
code of conduct as prescribed in the myth that good mothers are
all-caring and all-protecting.

> 'We're literally "protecting our children to death," and the fatal weap-
> ons we use are our big hearts, our ignorance, and the overwhelming
> desire to be a "good mother."

The prevailing myth of our culture says clutch your tender children tight and keep them safe from the world where harm lurks
everywhere. Worrywarts are revered as vigilant, wise, and caring
good mothers. In fact, if we let the leash loose, society sees us as
slack-happy moms not doing our jobs well.

Believe me—it is, in fact, the opposite. Pampering children is
often a quick and easy, shortsighted solution; it's much harder to do
the hard work of teaching, training, and guiding a child to manage
life independently and cooperatively with others. That's the slow
parenting way. But the long-term gains are worth it!

So let's see what exactly pampering is, look at how we came to
be so misguided as a culture, and explore the negative effects of
pampering. Then I'll give you two new parenting tools to work
with. You'll be doing less, and yet you'll be more effective. Family
life is about to get really good.

PAMPERING—WHAT ARE WE REALLY TALKIN' ABOUT HERE?

Let's make sure we all understand what exactly pampering is and how to spot it in our parenting before we plough in any deeper on the topic. In the most general sense, pampering describes the actions of adults (especially the iconic "good mother") that deny children their basic right to learn and grow as they are meant to!

The pampered child is given an alibi and is excused from facing life's challenges. They manage to avert the need to cooperate or take their rightful responsibilities, thanks to a willing adult accomplice who rescues them from this work.

Pampered children are exempt from making adjustments to fit into the workings of the greater social systems of the family and classroom. Instead they demand that the entire rest of the world move and adjust to accommodate their personal whims and wishes. Good mothers actually work to *mooooove* the world in line with their child's preferences. Life for a pampered child has been sterilized, and a clear, smooth path is swept for them. They are protected from reality and the demands it places on them. Ultimately, this means they are left inadequately prepared for life.

Telltale Signs of a Pampering Mom

Do you:

- *Routinely do things for your children that they are capable of doing for themselves?*
- *Take over your child's responsibilities?*
- *Cater to and provide special services or special treatments for your child?*
- *Go about arranging life so your little one is protected from having to experience life's routine knocks and blows?*

Still not sure? Here are some concrete examples of pampering that are fairly common in families. Do you do recognize any?

1. You sleep in your child's bed because she won't sleep without you there.
2. You indulge a picky eater and cook a separate meal for him (or do you just cut the crusts off and serve it up on *only* the yellow plate, as his highness prefers?).
3. You lie or cover up events to avoid upsetting your child. For example, replacing Swimmy with a look-alike fish, hoping your child won't notice her pet died.
4. You shout constant reminders to "watch out," "be careful," or simply "that's dangerous—let mommy do it."
5. You insist your child zip up his coat and wear a hat so he doesn't get cold. You know best when he's cold, don't you?
6. You pick up after your children since they refuse to, and you're tired of fighting about it.
7. You constantly spot your child money because she always seems to fall short.
8. You talk for your child.
9. You insist the school give your child the teacher he likes best, and also put his best friend in that class, too.
10. You buy a second version of everything you own so your children don't have to wait, share, or feel left out.

Did you answer yes to any of these? Pampering can be hard to notice if it's YOUR child and YOUR issue; it's so much easier to see in others. Yet, almost all of us are guilty of this ourselves.

WHY WE ARE A PAMPERING CULTURE?
There are several reasons why our society is so ripe to pamper its young, and they directly or indirectly affect all of us in our parenting styles. Let's take a moment to understand each of these factors.

Changes in Family Size: Hey, Where Did All the Kids Go?

We've come a long way from the old days when you married young and started producing children to help on the farm. Back then you had 14 children, knowing four or five would likely be taken by typhus, scarlet fever, consumption, or the plague of the day. Not anymore... Now we often wait until we are near the end of our natural reproductive years before we even try to start a family. We wait so long that we only have time to have one or two kids before our eggs expire and our chromosomes start to go funky. And besides—they cost too much now! Have you seen the price of private school and university tuition? Children used to be a commodity that added economic value to the family—free workers! This social trend of having fewer children later in life places special significance on each child, and adds to the general climate that supports this crazy notion of pampering our children.

The Cultural Belief That Our Children Are Not Able

Gandhi left school at 13 to marry. Cleopatra was ruling Egypt at 17. Why do we think 13-year-old Ben can't manage to do his own laundry? Or that at six Sarah still can't dress herself without us? Have humans evolved into less capable beings? Or, have we just lowered our expectations? As life expectancy has improved, we have been able to extend childhood longer. You don't need to be reproducing at 14 because you're going to be dead by 30. Phew! There certainly are some benefits to that! However, it does invite us to baby our children longer and longer. We rightly initiated child labor laws to keep kids out of the workforce, but now we can't even get this generation to take the garbage to the curb.

Children have not changed—our attitudes about them have. We have stopped asking children to contribute to the family. We've stopped training them to have skills, which means that over time, when we claim they're incapable, it's often because they have become so! We've plucked their wings, and then we wag the finger at their inability to fly.

Pampering Feels Good

Pampering just feels good for us moms. It feels so loving to care for someone. Sure, they keep growing and they could be a little more independent, but where would that leave us?

Out of a job.

We want to keep looking after them because it makes us feel, well, like a mother! And mothers are important, and needed. In fact, we enjoy having dependents because it proves our importance and gives us a sense of value, perhaps with a sprinkle of superiority throw on top. THEY CAN' T MANAGE WITHOUT US—WE ARE IMPORTANT!

"Put on your sweater—you'll be chilly" is really a testament to just how much we know, and how superior our judgment is. Here's a new concept: It's really none of our business! Not convinced that your six-year-old is capable of deciding when and where to put her coat on? She can, but we prefer to act under the guise of concern so we can set ourselves up to be superior to our children by being big, powerful, and all-protecting.

Who Are We Kidding? It's Easier!

And while we're looking at self-interested reasons for our pampering, let's not overlook the obvious: *It's easier.* If your child is screaming in the night, it's faster, easier, and a whole lot simpler for you to bring him into bed with you than to lose sleep while you train him to soothe himself back to sleep independently. If your child keeps calling from school saying she forgot her homework and that leaves you stuck driving it out to her, it's easier to just start checking her knapsack, isn't it? Well, it is—but only in the short term, as we'll see.

The Cultural Belief That Our Children Are Fragile and Vulnerable

Of special concern to moms is the crucial importance of developing a "secure attachment" between the child and primary caregiver in those first few years of life. I agree whole-heartedly. Bond away! But don't think for a moment that effective discipline and child guidance interferes with the ability to bond! We've got an entire league of mothers who are paralyzed from performing any discipline because with one tear shed, moms back down on their resolve to follow through, worried they're severing the attachment!

Let's set the record straight: The whole point of needing to bond and attach is to assure children they are loved, safe and secure. Proper discipline accomplishes that! The establishing of appropriate boundaries and limits—and the consistent enforcement of them in a friendly manner—helps children feel a sense of order in a life that might otherwise be chaos. Life begins to feel predictable. That predictability affords the child his sense of security.

The baby also needs to feel sure that her needs will be met. However, good mothers have no sense of the difference between a child's needs and her wants, or between what a child "can't do" and what he "won't do." Meeting our children's needs and helping them when they're incapable is our responsibility. Catering to demands and preferences is pampering.

Sarah left her nine-month-old with her mother, warning her that the baby still wakes and cries every few hours in the night. Sarah explains to grandma that the way to get the baby back to sleep is to sit with the baby on top of an exercise ball and bounce. When grandma went to the crying babe, she tried to resettle him by rocking in the rocking chair and then by walking, but the cries grew louder. Out of frustration she decided that she'd forget her arthritic hip and start bouncing. Just at that moment the baby gave her a big grin that said, "finally—you did what I wanted." This is the baby's preference, but it is uncooperative because it interferes with mother's (or grandma's) right to sleep. When mom doesn't address the sleep-training issues, she is pampering her child and protecting him from his job of adapting to a family that sleeps in the evening.

Children who don't sleep through the night by eight months are often still not sleeping through the night by four years. This is because the parents are unable to do the business of sleep training, and it is one of the first indicators of the parent's inability to manage child guidance and discipline. If you are a pampering parent, this is your first yellow flag! Learning to sleep without disturbing others is early training in cooperation, and concerns of severing attachments are a load of unwarranted fears.

It would be so much more helpful and useful for all of us to remember that our children and babies are wonderfully robust and truly capable. They can, in fact, manage life beautifully if we just offer some guidance and allow them a go at it! We must change our social climate to one that has faith in its children!

CHANGES IN PARENTING STYLES

To really get our heads around the phenomenon of pampering and the societal havoc it's creating in near epidemic proportions, we have to look at why our parenting styles have changed so drastically in recent years. Even beyond the factors mentioned earlier in this chapter, these really are interesting times in the history of parenting.

We've decided the old Archie Bunker style of autocratic parenting that has been the tradition for centuries and centuries is no longer how we want to parent. Well hallelujah for that.

However, in the removal of one dominant ideology, we find ourselves struggling—awaiting the new ideology of democratically run families to become firmly entrenched in society. This transitional period has resulted in most parents taking on a pampering style, and we'll see how easy it was to arrive there.

Autocratic parenting is a micro-model of the way all social institutions used to be organized: hierarchically. It's a pretty simple model to recognize. First you take one person, say a king or a father, and you make him the ruler. He gets to lord over people who have no say about his choices or how he got in power in the first place.

He uses his position of power to control the people beneath him who have very limited rights and powers. Of course, he still needs a way to get the people to actually *abide* by his rules. Because people do not like being ruled over, they could just scoff and say, "NO, I won't pay the royal taxes," or in the case of the family, "NO, I won't cut your lawn."

The king needs to be able to *make* the people abide by the rules, so he uses the threat of punishment, like beheadings or locking his subjects into stocks in the street. For refusing to cut the grass, maybe you'd settle for a "grounding." The ruler also uses rewards to entice people to do as he says. Money, sticker charts, status, and favoritism all work. At least, they work in the short term.

Either way, the people are manipulated into obedience or forced into compliance. They do not willingly cooperate when they're being subjugated to another's domination. Suffice it to say, the relationship is distant and strained.

Well, obviously, this model had some basic human rights violations. As society matures, we no longer want blind obedience. We want cooperative citizenship. Slowly, over time, we have been fighting towards social democratization of our nations, the workplace, and the family.

It's easy to forget that over the years people have fought with their lives to attain many things that we recognize now as being such basic rights:

- People are innocent until proven guilty.
- People have the right to own land.
- People have the right to vote their leaders into office.
- People have the right to be free from slavery.
- People have the right to be treated with dignity and respect regardless of race, color, creed, nationality, sexuality, or age.

Social equality: *Respecting the inherent dignity and worth of every human being.*

Out with the King?

In our excitement to honor children's rights and freedoms and to treat them respectfully, we try to parent in new ways. But just exactly what way is that? We know what NOT to do, but do we know what to do instead? Here's what happens: We end up putting the child's rights above our own, and now, ironically, the family is still arranged hierarchically, but with tyrant children ruling the house. We've overcompensated in our movement away from autocratic parenting, and as you're about to see, the results are just as damaging.

THE GROWTH-INHIBITING EFFECTS OF PAMPERING

To better understand the impact of pampering, let's try to step inside the world of the pampered child, and experience what it's like to be the recipient of this kind of attention and protection, and to be serviced by others. What is the child thinking? Feeling? What is the child deciding about himself, life, and strategies for living and coping in these pampered conditions?

Pampering Is Discouraging

Imagine if you were the little boy who one day notices that Swimmy looks different, and you find out that mom covered up his untimely demise. Mom's actions send the message that she doesn't think you can handle the reality of Swimmy's death.

Mom's pampering lets you know the low opinion she holds of you and your inabilities to face common challenges. You might think that if mom lacks faith in you, why would you think any differently about yourself? After all, mom is a bright respectable woman, and if she thinks you're incapable of handling emotional stress, well, maybe you *are* an emotional weakling.

Using Deficiencies to Our Benefit

Of course, there are always other ways children might interpret a situation for themselves. Look at Avery—he learned that if he didn't hold his bottle, his mother would; that if he didn't pick up his spoon to get the cereal in, his mother would; and that if he didn't work at tying up his shoes, his mother would do it for him.

Avery's trial-and-error learning taught him that being deficient at skills was sure a great way to get people engaged with you. He stopped trying to develop skills and instead learned the skill of charm, feigning he couldn't do things when he could and enlisting others to help him. Some adults, eventually his girlfriends and later his fiancée, would care for him in a way that made them feel good too, in a co-dependency kind of way.

All in all, Avery learned how to feel important through dependency. Since this is all he knows, he organizes life to keep this pattern of relationships going, because it's familiar and comfortable to him. Ahhh, see? We love predictability to make us feel secure, even when it's unhealthy.

Different Rules for Me

If mother always allowed you to sleep in her bed while others were left to sleep alone, if mother always carried you while everyone else was made to walk, and if mother made you a special meal while others ate the standard fare, it would be easy to see how you may deduce that since all these exceptions to the rule are made especially and only for you, well—gosh, I guess you must be thinking that you *are* special!

Children who feel "special" because the rules have been altered for them, often come to decide that, in general, NO rules apply to them. After all, they are "special" and above the rules.

Paul, pampered by his mom for his whole 12 years of life, has never had to accommodate or be a team player. Every discomfort or problem he has ever faced, his mother solved on his behalf.

On his first trip to summer camp, Paul was up against life without mom for the first time. Apparently, dealing with camp food was more than poor pampered Paul could take.

You see, at home Paul's mom acts as his short-order cook. In the dining hall, after turning up his nose at the evening meal, Paul marched into the kitchen demanding they make him a cheese sandwich instead. They explained that they couldn't do that: "Imagine if we did that for everyone?" He became irate—furious that life was not amenable to his wishes.

When he asked his counselor if he could phone home and have his mom bring him some food or snacks, he was told that it was against the rules to have your own outside food. Paul was indignant: "Don't they understand? I *can't* eat this." Paul is accustomed to getting his way. He has no tolerance for when things don't go his way, no interest outside of himself.

Paul did phone home—to ask to be picked up ten days before session was over! That was the end of his camp experience. Too bad. Paul had the opportunity to build strong friendships and join his cabin mates as they all laughed together at the oatmeal that could be sliced into bricks. He could have toiled and struggled with KP duty and sweeping up the cabin, felt the sense of pride and accomplishment for a job done well, and a sense of belonging that can only be achieved from participating and contributing and giving of one's self for others' benefit.

But Paul has come to believe that he is above the common rules. He feels devalued and put out when he's asked to do what all others are required to do. Will Paul ignore other rules—school rules? Speed limits? Maybe he'll decide he's above societal rules and become a petty thief. Our juvenile detention centers are full of pampered children. But then again, so are our counseling offices, mental-health facilities, drug rehab clinics, and so forth. It's a costly societal problem to not want to join others and cooperate.

Pampered Children Feel Special and Superior

We want all children to feel special in a "you're unique and important just the way you are" sort of way, but we *don't* want children to feel a sense of "specialness" that makes them feel superior or above others.

In order to feel superior, you must have some way of measuring and evaluating the people around you. That evaluation process is what makes us judgmental as humans, and it creates the exact conditions that stimulate a competitive rather than a cooperative approach to relationships.

When we feel we're "above others," we're no longer equals, and we lose that wonderful connection equality affords. It's true—it IS lonely at the top! Many people who feel they are superior also suffer great loneliness and depression that arises from a lack of connection and belonging with others.

People can have many friends and acquaintances but still feel disconnected, or distant. That distance comes not only when feeling "below" or inadequate compared to others, but also when we feel superior and elevated. The human heart and psyche longs to be elbow to elbow, toiling with our fellow man!

Think about it: How can children get along with others if we pit them again each other, teaching them to dominate and subvert each other in order to maintain the special status that we've bestowed on them?

Self-Righteous Entitlement

If you have always gotten your own way in life, you might come to expect it as your right. You get angry when you don't get your way, as if you now have suddenly been punished. You have not developed your social interest, which is the capacity to participate in the give-and-take needed to be in harmonious relationships with people, friends, lovers, and spouses.

The pampered child also misses out on crucial learning and developing. Mom's interference actually prevents them from developing their abilities to manage life, so they end up with this odd combination of feeling entitled yet also feeling rather useless. This is a very common experience among children today.

Poor Self-Concept

It is through the experience of facing challenges and successfully overcoming them that we develop a positive self-concept. We grow our abilities and develop more and more strengths and competencies, and this helps build our own attitude of self-love and pride. Pampering stunts these opportunities for self-esteem development.

I'LL JUST PAMPER FOR A FEW YEARS—EARLY CHILDHOOD IS THE TIME YOU NEVER GET BACK!

Even with all this new knowledge about pampering, where it comes from, and how it can be detrimental, it can *still* be a tough pitch to convince a pampering mother to give up her ways.

Let me share with you my all-time favorite pampering story. It took place during a workshop, when a mother in the audience asked me for help with the battle she had been having every single morning with getting her son up and ready for school on time. After all, his dawdling was making her late for work every day!

How could she get him in the car on time?

Everyone was eager to hear my advice because this is such a universal issue with our children. After hearing the details of how her morning went, we started into strategies. Well, at some point she interrupted to correct me: "Oh, no—actually he's not getting a drive to 'school,' he goes to college." Everyone was thrown! There was no way you could tell from her son's behavior and her treatment of him that she'd been talking about a grown man. Her son was 20 years old, living at home, and acting like a child who still needed his mommy to manage the morning routine. She willingly serviced him. She fought to wake him up, pushed him to eat breakfast, and then dealt with his dawdling to the car so she could chauffeur him to his college campus. All this so he wouldn't have to face the horrid reality of ... da da da dum ... public transit!

Every person in that workshop knew in that very moment that if they didn't stop pampering their children and managing their morning routines NOW—this was a picture of their future! She taught my workshop lesson better than I ever could have.

WHAT **CAN** WE DO?

So here we find ourselves in this most interesting of times. We don't know how to parent in a new style, and yet we don't want to be autocratic and punitive like in the past. We're stuck!

Here's how parenting today most often looks:

You try calling politely for Jake to come to supper. You want to treat him respectfully. Truly, you do. But when he ignores you and does not stop playing—what then? Supper is getting cold on the table, and you start thinking that old autocratic way is looking mighty fine again. Now Jake's freedom to play is interfering with YOU! Now he is being disrespectful to your time and the work you put into preparing supper.

Without the use of punishments and rewards to manipulate him, pray tell, how *do* we get Jake to come for supper? Mom feels she has only two choices, screaming at him in the old autocratic way, or giving up and letting Jake eat whenever it bloody well suits him. Seems he has no need to make adjustments or to cooperate with the family. When he comes in later, he'll just ask mom for supper then, and because it is his "right" to eat and he "needs" food, mom will offer him up food on his private timeline. Well, this is

Jake being pampered, and mom can't see a way around it with out being rude or mean. But there is. Let me show you.

THE DEMOCRATIC MODEL: THE ALTERNATIVE

The democratic model reminds us that no one is a slave to another. We are all free, and with that freedom comes responsibility.

> *Homework Assignment: Worried that if you treat your children as capable equals they'll run amuck with all that freedom? Would they rather run wild, without any rules at all? Try it—for a week!*
>
> *I have given this homework assignment to many families over the years. Try living as a family without structure for one week. You'll need to explain to the children that if they are allowed to live freely, then mom and dad are, too. The same rules should apply to all in a democracy. Everyone should be free to do as they please for a week. It only takes a couple of days before children start moaning for order! Why haven't we had any meals? I have no clean clothes! Why didn't you pick me up after soccer practice? What do mean you didn't feel like it?*
>
> *The children of this family will quickly understand the many benefits of order. They'll see that it is in everyone's interest to make agreements that help us live with **some** order as we arrange our lives together. These arrangements allow us to function. We call this "the ironclad logic of social living."*

In the democratic model, parents have different roles to play, with different responsibilities and duties than children, but they are not superior to their children. They are not using power and domination to achieve control, but instead they are winning the cooperation of others based on the ironclad laws of social living amongst equals. Everyone has a say, but you may not always get your way. The new authority in the family is the "social order," or the agreements you make together. This model respects our children's right to make choices, but it also holds them responsible for the outcomes of their choices.

Jake was called for supper. He chose not to come. That is his choice—mom can't *make* him. But Jake is choosing to miss supper when he doesn't come to the family meal. If he is hungry, it is his decision to skip the meal and he must bear the weight of his choice by being hungry 'til the next meal. It is not respectful of the order of the house or of mom's time to expect her to accommodate him. Mom is only responsible for setting out the meal as she agreed. No more, no less. She is not responsible for him and his choices. She does not need to take on the job of "nag" to get him to come in, nor does she need to cook and clean again later to service him. Perhaps Jake, knowing that not coming when called results in his having to wait to eat until the morning (or getting his own meal and cleaning it up so his mom isn't inconvenienced), might just make his own decision to join the family and reap the benefits of being a team player!

BYE BYE PAMPERING: THE DEMOCRATIC PARENT'S FIRST TOOLS

Jake just learned a lot, and he'll probably not miss another supper. He is now motivated to come to supper, and he doesn't rely on his mom to get him there. How could all that change have been brought about without mom giving a lecture? How did he learn?

Jake experienced what we call a "logical consequence"—missing out on having supper with his family, and also a natural consequence—hunger from no food! These are a parent's first tools that we need to learn about in guiding a child in a democracy.

The overprotecting mom can help her child to gain some growth-inducing experiences in life by allowing her child to experience the consequences of his actions. The metaphor I've heard that captures this so beautifully is to think of ourselves not as a maternal windblock, but instead to function as life's sieve, allowing our children to experience that which we filter to them. We can present challenges that are just within their grasp. They can then use their strengths and gradually build up their abilities and psychological muscle to allow them to confront more and more. This begins the day they are born.

From that first day forward, children are experiential learners, and they will need you to help them learn about the two types of laws that govern their world:

1. The natural world and its laws.
2. The social world with its social conventions.

Natural Consequences

The word *consequence* refers to outcomes. In teaching our children about natural consequences, we are helping them tie together in their minds the idea of cause and effect, the idea that we can change outcomes by changing our behaviors.

Natural consequences work quickly and clearly. The basic idea is that whenever Mother Nature can do the teaching—take a step back and let her do it for you! Your first task is to simply stand back and ask yourself if you need to do *anything*. What happens if you simply let your child deal with life as it unfolds? Less mothering for you!

Annie wanted to swim in the new wading pool mom had filled in the backyard with the garden hose. Mom told Annie, "No—the water is too cold, you can go in when it warms up." Annie and mom fought about going in for two hours until finally, out of frustration, mom said, "Fine! Go in." Annie got on her bathing suit, put one leg over the edge and, on feeling the water with her foot, decided she'd wait 'til it was warmer.

GOOD MOTHERS ARE ALL-CARING AND ALL-PROTECTING

Mom did not have to protect Annie from the cold water. She was not in danger. Mom created a two-hour ordeal for no reason, except perhaps her instinct to prove her superior wisdom to her daughter. Mom could have simply replied, "It's too cold for my liking, but you can decide for yourself." This shows faith in and respect for her daughter and her daughter's ability to decide for herself.

The same applies to Jake and eating. Jake can miss a meal. He will experience the natural consequence of hunger. He may feel uncomfortably hungry, but again, he is not in danger. Children need to learn the connection between food and hunger, and then figure out how much to eat to make it through to the next meal. "Good mothers" don't trust their own children to know their bodies. They think they know better. Well, in fact, most parents grossly overestimate the amount their children need to eat, and often still push them to "clean their plate." We train children to NOT listen to their body's cues and to listen to us instead.

Children have growth spurts and eat like bears getting ready to hibernate, and then, if they're about to come down with a bug or cut a tooth, they lose their appetite for days. The point is, trust that children can decide on how much to eat for themselves. Your job is to buy healthy food and serve it on a regular and predicable schedule. It's the child's job to eat, to figure out how much to eat, and to make the appropriate adaptation to fit into the family routines of eating.

Somewhere in all that figuring you know they're going to make some misjudgments and sure, they will wind up getting hungry. If you scramble to get them food, you are pampering. They will not learn to adjust themselves if you adjust for them. If you have empathy and tell them you know they'll make it to the next meal, you are allowing them to learn from natural consequences and to be intrinsically motivated to make alternate choices next time. They adapt—the social order stays the same. Ta da—training for co-operation.

Reminders for Using the Parenting Technique of Natural Consequences

Of course, we don't use natural consequences when the outcome is too harsh or dangerous. We don't teach about traffic by having our kids playing in the street! But if you have a tendency to pamper, you're going to have to remind yourself that a paper cut, splinter, bumped knee, or even a split lip and a few stitches are not damaging or dangerous.

Also, this technique won't work if the consequence is not experienced immediately. For example, the natural consequence of not brushing your teeth is tooth decay, but it will take years for the consequence to appear. A child will never connect the dots between those events, and you don't have the benefit of ten years to train for dental hygiene. Thankfully, there are many non-punitive tools in the democratic parenting toolbox.

Logical Consequences

Logical consequences teach social rules. They work in much the same way as natural consequences, but they require some thinking on mom's part to determine exactly what the logical consequence is in any given situation.

> *A good logical consequence must be:*
> - **Logical**—*to the child.*
> - **Related**—*to the child's actions. (Not coming for supper resulting in no TV makes no sense.)*
> - **Respectful**—*always! We're talking about people here.*
> - **Revealed in Advance**—*the child needs to know the outcomes of each option in advance of making a decision.*

The trick is to try to have the logical consequence unfold just as consistently and as matter-of-factly as a natural consequence, with no lecture, no frowns of disappointment, and no judgment of any kind.

Cathy kept leaving her bike on the driveway, and dad had to stop the car and move it every time he came home. Dad explained that part of owning and operating a bike is also the responsibility of caring for it and putting it away properly. Dad let Cathy know that if he found the bike on the driveway again, it would tell him that she's not interested in looking after her bike, and he'd lock it up for a week. She could try again at the end of the week.

When dad pulled in three days later and the bike was out, he didn't say a word to Cathy—he simply followed through, firm and friendly, with the logical consequence. Cathy now understands when she sees the bike gone and the car in the driveway. No words were exchanged, and it never happened again.

Tips for Success!

Are you ready to try applying some logical consequences? If so, let me remind you of a few pointers:

1. You must follow through, and I don't just mean the first time, but each and every time. Consistency is one of the keys to learning. Help your children to learn quickly by being consistent yourself. If the consequence for getting up and down from the table is that your plate is removed and you miss the rest of the meal, you must do this every time! In three days you'll have the benefit of a nice family meal with no interruptions.

2. Children don't learn from the threat of a consequence, they learn from experiencing it. Read that sentence again because it seems to get missed by so many people. Most pampering moms just threaten what they are going to do and never follow through. Kids know this about you, so you'll be ineffective with this method if you don't stop talking and TAKE ACTION—just lock the bike, take the plate, and so on.
3. Watch the attitude. If you do this with any kind of judgment, you won't be effective, you'll just invite a power struggle. The idea is that the situational needs and logical outcomes are responsible for how this is unfolding—it's nothing personal. You need to be uninterested in the choices your children make for themselves.

THROWING OFF THE SHACKLES OF DEPENDENCE

Take the pledge. Repeat after me: I will never do for a child what a child can do for him- or herself. This pledge is the gift you give your children when you actively decide to no longer be their willing accomplice in the pampering. Instead, today we liberate you both to throw off the shackles of dependence and invite you to let your children enjoy the benefits of learning to use their strengths to manage life's ever-growing challenges.

Children who can manage themselves are not only self-confident, but can also use their talents to contribute to the family's operating. This is critical. Children feel their sense of connection and belonging as a result of participating and contributing to the family. We call these the "P and C's" for short. These tasks help nurture children's social interest and, again—it's less for you to do!

Moms are often at a loss for knowing just what are reasonable expectations for their children. I have provided a list below that is by no means definitive, but it will provide you with some benchmarks and give you lots of ideas about what else your children may be ready to tackle:

GOOD MOTHERS ARE ALL-CARING AND ALL-PROTECTING

Responsibilities for a Two- to Three-Year-Old
- Pick up unused toys and put in the proper place.
- Put books and magazines in a rack.
- Sweep the floor.
- Place napkins, plates, and silverware on the table. (The silver is on but not correctly at first.)
- Tidy up what they drop after eating.
- Make simple decisions (e.g., as when given a choice of two foods for breakfast).
- Use the toilet.
- Simple hygiene—brush teeth, wash and dry hands, and brush hair.
- Undress self, and dress with some help.
- Carry boxed or canned goods from the grocery sacks to the proper shelf. Put some things away on a lower shelf.
- Clear own place at the table. Put the dishes on the counter after cleaning any leftovers off the plate.

Responsibilities for a Four-Year-Old
- Set the table.
- Help put the groceries away.
- Help with grocery shopping and compile a grocery list.
- Follow a schedule for feeding pets.
- Help do simple yard and garden work.
- Help make the beds and vacuum.
- Help do the dishes or fill the dishwasher.
- Learn responsibilities by making a goal chart (with your help). Then if the work is done all week, the parents and child get take part in an enjoyable activity.
- Spread butter on sandwiches.
- Prepare cold cereal.
- Help parent prepare plates of food for the family dinner.

- Make a simple dessert (e.g., add topping to cupcakes or Jell-O, pour the toppings on ice cream).
- Hold the hand mixer to whip potatoes or mix up a cake.
- Share toys with friends (practice courtesy and sharing).
- Get the mail.
- Be able to play without constant adult supervision and attention.
- Hang socks, handkerchiefs, and wash clothes on a lower line.
- Bring the milk from the fridge.
- Sharpen pencils.

Responsibilities for a Five- to Six-Year-Old
- Help with the meal planning and grocery shopping.
- Make own sandwich or simple breakfast, then clean up.
- Pour own drink.
- Tear up lettuce for a salad.
- Put in certain ingredients in a recipe.
- Make bed and clean room.
- Dress self and choose outfit for the day.
- Scrub the sink, toilet, and bathtub.
- Clean mirrors and windows.
- Separate clothing for washing. Put white clothes in one separate pile and colors in another.
- Fold clean clothes and put them away.
- Answer the telephone and dial the phone for use.
- Yard work.
- Pay for small purchases.
- Take out the garbage.
- Feed pets and clean their living area.

GOOD MOTHERS ARE ALL-CARING AND ALL-PROTECTING

Responsibilities for a Seven-Year-Old
- Oil and care for bike, and lock it and put it away when unused.
- Take phone messages and write them down.
- Run simple errands for parents.
- Water the lawn.
- Wash dog or cat.
- Carry in the grocery sacks.
- Get self up in the morning with an alarm clock. Do own preparations for bedtime and then involve parent.
- Learn to be polite, courteous, and to share; respect others.
- Carry own lunch money and notes back and forth to school.
- Leave the bathroom in order; hang up clean towels.

Responsibilities for an Eight- to Nine-Year-Old
- Fold napkins properly and set silverware properly.
- Mop the floor.
- Help rearrange furniture. Help plan the layout.
- Run own bath water.
- Help others with their work when asked.
- Straighten own closet and drawers.
- Shop for and select own clothing and shoes with parents.
- Fold blankets.
- Sew buttons.
- Sew rips in seams.
- Clean up animal "messes" in the yard and house.
- Begin to read recipes and cook for the family.
- Babysit for short periods of time with adults present.
- Paint fence or shelves.
- Help write simple letters.[1]

---

1 Adapted from a handout by Marion Balla, Adlerian Counselling and Consulting Centre, Ottawa.

You will need to spend time teaching and mentoring your children around each of these new skills. Be sure to be precise: "When it's your job to wash the mirror the bathroom, you need to get the Windex and paper towels, which are kept under the sink. Spray about five or six squirts and then take about this much paper towel and start rubbing. See how it's streaky in the beginning? We need to keep rubbing, and then we need to do it in a formation so the streaks don't show. When all the streaks are gone, the mirror is done! The dirty paper towels go in the kitchen garbage, not the decorative bathroom wastebasket, and the supplies go back under the sink."

That may sound long and painful, but a five year-old needs to know the new skill, the expectations, and the entirety of the project.

HANDING OVER RESPONSIBILITY: WHAT TO EXPECT

There are probably a ton of responsibilities you know your child can do with no training—you just need to step back. Now that you're psyched to do some "letting go," let's make sure you understand that your children will not jump into perfect action when taking on a new responsibility. It's a process. I think if you understand the stages, you'll be less apt to think things are not working out. Patience is a virtue here. Remember, this is slow parenting with long-term payoffs.

1. *Disbelief stage*: They don't really think that you'll follow through with letting them manage on their own.
2. *Testing stage*: They will enjoy checking for your reactions, testing to see how long you can go before you jump in and take over again.
3. *Belief stage*: With repeated experience of you not stepping in and not taking over or rescuing them, and by allowing them to experience the consequence of their

choices, they will start to understand that no one else has a vested interest in their situation except them!

4. *Mistakes stage*: When children finally decide that it's in their own best interest to look after their own responsibilities, and that no one else is going to make this happen but them, they will start to figure out how to solve this problem for themselves. Being a neophyte at it, they will make errors in judgment and strategies. They will screw up quite a bit during this particular stage. This is when parents must resist the urge to take over or rescue. Instead, you can coach them to success by a using "appreciative inquiry" or Socratic-style questions. Notice how the mother leads the child to think for him- or herself by only asking questions and not solving the child's problem:

- "Seems your plan for looking after your swimming gear didn't work out. What happened?"
- "What could you do to remind yourself that Tuesdays are swimming days?"
- "Seems leaving a note on the door didn't work for you this time. What would you like try differently next time?"

5. *Competence*: This is the stage parents want so badly, but they have to be patient and realize it is the last of five stages. It does come eventually. While it may cost the child a few missed swimming classes or other such inconveniences and disappointments, it's worth it!

If you started this chapter as a pampering mom who loved to do for her children, I hope you were able to get in touch with the origins of your own myths about the need to nurture in order to be a good mother. I hope you will embrace all those loving parts of you that contribute positively to being in a great relationship with your children, while working to minimize the growth-inhibiting prospect of overdoing and pampering such that your children miss out on their own development. We need both firm and friendly in our parenting. I hope you feel inspired to create this balance in your own style.

For some of us, the need to be loving and friendly isn't the trouble; it's our propensity toward firmness and control. If you're a zero-tolerance parent and feel it's your job to control your children, then read on—this next chapter is for you!

CHAPTER 5

MYTH:
GOOD MOTHERS ARE IN CONTROL

GOOD MOTHERS ARE IN CONTROL

> *"Control is never achieved when sought after directly. It is the surprising outcome of letting go."*
>
> —James Arthur Ray

J anice expressly told her daughter, Samantha, that the chocolate-chip granola bars were for school lunches only, and *not* for snacking on at home. When she found a wrapper between the cushions of the couch, she realized her tenacious five-year-old was sneaking them behind her back. The nerve! So after another stern talking to, she moved the granola bars to the cupboard above the fridge, out of Samantha's reach. But the next day she walked into the kitchen only to discover a dining room chair pushed over to the counter: her daughter was scaling up the fridge!

Oh yeah, it's war, baby, it's war!

LOSING THE BATTLE FOR DEMOCRATIC PARENTING

Do you feel your home is a battlefield of opposing wills, fraught with arguments and fights? Does every trip to the park have to end in a hostile toddler-takeover, as you finally throw her over your shoulder screaming and flailing? Or, does the open defiance of your 13-year-old make you think the teen years might best be spent at military school? Just wait 'til you see what the *sergeant* has to say about boys wearing their pants halfway down their butt and showing their BVDs to the world. Ha!

Don't start packing that trunk just yet ...

This chapter is for the mother who has the kind of child that you'd describe as "willful" or "spirited." Or perhaps you go with the more traditional moniker: "little shit." It's a chapter for *any* of us who find ourselves spending too much time feeling angry with our children, or feeling we don't deserve the crap we're constantly putting up with. It is also for us "good mothers" who no doubt feel on some level like we're failing as a mother because we're raising this child who is hard to control.

In the last chapter we looked at the trouble of moms who pamper, tipping the scale too far towards the "friendly" aspects of our firm and friendly model of parenting, and raising children who learn to live life in a parasitic fashion on an all-too-willing host: mother. Now we'll check in with moms with the opposite tendency: the "firm" moms. An affinity for firmness usually means that while trying to establish and enforce limits and boundaries, "friendly" goes out the window and we come off as being controlling and dominating, as establishing too many rules, and as overusing our personal (and often arbitrary) authority over our children.

Are You a Closet Controller?

1. *Do your children accuse you of sticking your nose in their business too much?*

2. *Do you feel you just want to be helpful by showing your child a way to do things that's better? More efficient?*

3. *Do your children accuse you of being bossy?*

4. *Do your children argue that you just don't understand them? That you can't see things from their perspectives?*

5. *Do you find yourself overburdened with tasks because you prefer things a certain way, and it's just easier to do it yourself?*

6. *Do you feel uncomfortable when others are doing things that you feel could be done in a better (read: "the right") way?*

Some of us were control freaks before we had children, but for many it reared its ugly head only when we become mothers.

In order to bust this myth, first we'll investigate control and our desire for it, and see how in trying to gain control we inadvertently lose it. Then I'll show you how to gain the firmness you seek with techniques that are democratic and aimed at winning your children's cooperation instead of winning a battle over them.

HOW CONTROL GETS IN THE WAY

Take-charge people can be wonderfully accomplished taskmasters, scholars, and high achievers. I am sure you all have lovely, well-organized kitchens and no doubt your underwear and sock drawers have been arranged according to the Dewey decimal system. But they often pay a price in their personal relationships, because human beings don't like to be controlled by others. It usurps their personal power. Children are no exception—but of course you've probably already discovered that the hard way.

The traditional autocratic parent–child relationship is *defined* by the superior–inferior arrangement of power in the family, with the belief that parents must wield power over the children in order to make them mind the rules. Many people still desire to raise their children by this method. The trouble is, it's no longer working.

Why Doesn't It Work Anymore?

Today's kids no longer feel socially inferior to adults and they won't tolerate being forced into that inferior position. When the women's movement took hold, children began arriving into egalitarian households rather then hierarchical ones. Now that men and women are (fairly) equal, children don't perceive a social pecking order as they did in the past. Society is embracing equality and doing a better job of treating children as social equals as well. We no longer see spanking in public (not that it doesn't occur at home) and the strap has been abolished from the school system. Children are no longer to be "seen and not heard." Most kids today feel their own sense of social equality, whether parents are prepared for this or not.

So what happens when you impose old-world autocratic parenting techniques on a new generation of children who feel you're equals? They rebel. We try to use control as our method of discipline, to make our children mind, but often all we end up with are huge power struggles.

We have discussed the idea that all human behavior serves a purpose and that under the age of ten there are four basic goals of children's misbehaviors; attention, power, revenge, and avoidance. These are behaviors that solve a problem for children. The child who finds himself in power struggles has found a way to attain power through means of battling with you. A child *needs* power. In a democracy, living as a social equal, everyone has a right to have a say about those things that impact him or her. When children feel empowered, feel they have a say, they have found their power through these constructive avenues. Failing the ability to feel empowered in a positive way, children will struggle to overcome their feelings of powerlessness through unconstructive means.

For children there are two payoffs in the power struggle. The first is that they can make you angry. THAT feels pretty powerful to a kid! To rattle the cage of their parents and upset them makes kids feel big. The second payoff is that often when we engage in power struggles with children, the children win and get their way. If a child tantrums to stay up late, and you say—FINE, just ten more minutes—the child has learned that a tantrum is effective! And no child will abandon a behavior that is useful.

Of course, parents are bigger and they sometimes win the power struggles, too. The toddler thrown over your shoulder and hauled away angrily loses the power struggle, but the child is still learning from your modeling to try to get her way with other people through domination and control, as opposed to through cooperation. If power wielding is the model in the family, the child is apt to practice this herself, either with the parents, a younger sibling, or with other children on the schoolyard.

I have never met a power-hungry child that didn't have a power-hungry adult somewhere nearby.

The term "power struggle" has become a part of everyday language, and people know precisely what I'm talking about when I suggest that perhaps the reason their lovely 18-month-old corkscrews himself into a knot when they're attempting to change his diaper is because there is a power struggle going on. "Oh, yes! It's a power struggle for sure," they agree. But some power struggles are more subtle and difficult to detect. We need to be able to sense power struggles in all their forms, and we need a full understanding of the human dynamics involved in a power struggle if we're going to learn how to avert them.

UNDERSTANDING THE DYNAMICS OF A POWER STRUGGLE

In every relationship the distribution of power can be thought of as being in one of the two styles we've discussed:

1. *Vertical power arrangement.* Vertical power relationships are arranged in a one-up/one-down fashion. Since nobody enjoys being in the inferior, one-down position, we strive to attain the only other position available: one-up. From that vantage point, we dominate and control those people below to ensure we keep this position secured.
2. *Horizontal power arrangement.* Thankfully, there is an alternative. The dichotomy of superior/inferior is avoided when we see power as being shared amongst all people, and when we are not concerned with feelings of inferiority. We don't seek to have power over people, but instead to use our power to conquer common problems.

A power struggle is a phenomenon isolated to those who seek vertical power over others.

Power struggles would be better understood if we were to rename them "power contests." When we enter a contest, we are setting ourselves up to compete with an opponent, with a desire to have an outcome that deems one person a winner and one person a loser. The format itself is about determining who will be going up a rung on that vertical ladder and who is going down.

This idea is best exemplified by the old camp favorite—the tug of war. In the tug of war contest, you have two teams who are on opposite ends of a rope. Both teams are using all their power and might to defy the power and might of their opponent by pulling in opposing directions. The winner is the one who can outpower the other, causing them to lose ground and eventually be pulled to the winner's side. Fun, eh?

Lets see how we play "tug of war" with our children (all the time!) in the form of power struggles:

1. *It takes two to play.* You can't have a tug of war unless you have two people who agree to play. One person walking around with a rope just isn't the same. It only becomes a struggle when the other party picks up the rope and creates the opposing force. Game on! You play this together. It's a co-created dynamic—if you're engaged, angry, and fighting, you've willingly picked up the rope!

2. *Both parties have to be in opposition.* You can't be on the same team and have a power struggle. Someone has to be in opposition! You have to say YES so your child can say NO! You have to say RED cup so they can say BLUE cup.

And if you say "okay, blue cup," notice how quickly they re-vert to demanding the red cup again. Being in opposition is one method of showing you are strong and powerful. If I asked you to impress me with the strength of your biceps, you would not show me a limp arm at your side; you would roll up your sleeve and bend your arm, cre-ating opposition by pushing on your wrist so you get a nice, big, bulging muscle happening. Children who feel they need to look big are often looking for opposition to push against to show their strength and power. YOU provide that opposition.

3. *Winner/loser outcomes.* Remember that the whole goal of the game is to determine a winner and a loser and that the contest is over POWER. The outcome of the game dictates who is the master, who is the slave—who is the puppet master, who is the puppet.

All too often we get distracted by the details, thinking the child re-ally is fighting with us about the blue cup, or really is just trying to avoid the diaper change. Parents get perplexed and frustrated try-ing to solve the uninteresting questions: "Why does the cup color matter?" "Who wants to walk around in a poop-filled diaper?"

That is not the point of the fight. The fight is about domination and control. The cup color and diaper become the flag on the rope that allows us to decide who wins and who loses: "If I get to those granola bars from above the fridge, I have conquered mother's at-tempts to control me."

"DON'T WORRY—I'M NOT CONTROLLING"

It's very common for moms to be perceived as controlling even when they don't intend to exert control. You think it's nothing to simply say, "Put on your coat, it's time to go." However, to a child this statement can feel like a command rather than a request. You're *telling* me to put on my coat—NOW! Imagine if you were in the middle of a glass of wine and telling a story at a dinner party, and your husband said the same thing to you? It would feel very controlling to you then, too. The child now perceives that if he puts on his coat he would be acting obediently, and that feels like being in the inferior, one-down position. He will fight it. In the child's attempt to not feel like an underling, he refuses to put on his coat and the power struggle is on!

Because a sense of equality is lacking between the mother and child, the child views life as arranged vertically, with superiors and inferiors, so now the child vies to be in the superior position over you!

Once you have engaged in the power struggle, and both people are holding the rope, you have established that putting on the coat is the losing proposition. Think about it: How can he put on his coat without feeling like he has lost to you? Power struggles, once initiated, actually taint the very thing we want our children to do as unpalatable to them! We are at cross-purposes to our goal. If we want the jacket on, we had better not get into a power struggle about it. It lessens the likelihood of our eliciting cooperation.

GETTING OUT OF POWER STRUGGLES

Learning how to avert power struggles is going to take some work. Don't get discouraged during the learning process. I'm asking you to shift the dynamics of you family towards a more democratic model, with shared power and more respectful egalitarian relationships. Switching to the horizontal plan is a massive and all-encompassing change, and it won't happen overnight. You will start seeing *some* results right away, but manage your expectations and allow yourself six months to a year to fully accomplish this adjustment. Just remind yourself this is slow parenting, and know that you and your children will reap the rewards of your efforts, I promise.

We're taking a two-pronged approach. The short prong deals with how to get out of the immediate power struggle once you've already begun to play. The second prong is the longer term: how to help our children find power in the family in constructive ways, and how to include them in the decision making and functioning of the family such that they help create the agreements and rules they are expected to live by.

SHE'S SCALING UP THAT FRIDGE, WHAT AM I SUPPOSED TO BE DOING NOW?

I have a four-step model to help parents who find themselves in power struggles. Following these steps will move you away from the conflict state and towards winning cooperation instead of winning the fight.

In essence, what the parent must do is simple: DROP THE ROPE. You can't continue a power struggle if you're not willing to play. By dropping the rope, the game ends in a truce.

> 'We don't want to win the struggle because it only serves to model power struggles to our children and it means we are making losers out of our children, which is disrespectful to them.
>
> 'Neither do we want to lose the power struggle, because that is disrespectful to ourselves, and serves to show the child that power struggles are effective in getting your own way.
>
> So both winning and losing serve to sustain the use of power struggles in your family. 'Instead we need a different outcome. 'We need to call a truce, decline the invitation to fight, and drop the rope.

To drop the rope, follow these four steps in the D.R.O.P. model of moving from conflict to cooperation:

- **Detect** that you are in a power struggle.
- **Redefine** the roles and responsibilities for each person.
- **Offer** the olive branch and create choices.
- **Push** on positively doing what YOU are supposed to be doing.

Now let's look at each step in detail.

D—Detect That You Are in a Power Struggle

This is always the first step. We need to be aware that we are actually in a power struggle if we are to get out of it, which means we must determine that the child's goal is indeed power.

Power comes in two forms: *passive* and *active*. We seem to recognize the active form easily in our children. This is the child who is saying with her behavior: "I can do what I want." This child is actively playing the game of tug of war, and you know you have a talented opponent. The passive-power child, on the other hand, is harder to recognize. The passive-power child is also in the tug-of-war game, but instead of pulling madly, he is like the team anchor—on the end with the rope tied at his waist, feet firmly planted, and not budging. He sits like a rock, showing you his power by proving "you can't make me."

These are the ways we see active and passive power in our children:

Active Power
- Tantrums
- Open defiance
- Blow-ups

Passive Power
- They say they will, but they don't
- Laziness and sloppiness
- Lateness and dawdling
- Compliance with defiance

Are You in a Power Struggle?

*Clue #1—**Your feelings**: Are you angry, provoked, challenged, or defeated? Thinking: "You are not getting away with this!"*

*Clue #2—**Your typical response**: Do you yell, fight, and force them to mind?*

*Clue #3—**Your child's typical response to you**: Are they retrenching, fighting back harder, and escalating the conflict?*

In order to determine that power is your child's goal, and that you are indeed in a power struggle, check in with your emotional state. Do you feel angry? That's usually the most prominent emotion. We generate anger as the fuel to help us fight and conquer. You're getting pumped up to win the tug-of-war game.

Now tune in to the self-talk in your head. Does it sound something like "You're not getting away with this—I'll put locks on those cupboards if I have to!" or "I'll show *you*, young lady"? These are escalating, fighting thoughts that reflect the need to dominate, conquer, and regain a sense of control. If you're thinking thoughts like this, you can bet that your child's self-talk is exactly the same! (Where did they learn that?)

Lastly, if you're yelling and fighting with the child, and if the child responds to you by escalating the fight, you've got a power struggle on your hands.

R—Redefining Roles and Responsibilities

When we are embroiled in a power struggle, we are invested in having the situation turn out "our way." Having things turn out our own way is laden with the desire for personal power. "Good mothers" can be blind to this because of their belief that their way is also the RIGHT way, and hence they feel they are fighting for a true cause. Right should triumph over wrong. This desire for "rightness" compels us to micromanage our children. We repeatedly overstep our bounds and take over the child's roles and responsibilities. Children experience this as trespassing, and they fight to regain their rightful role.

Catherine had a two-year-old with eating issues. Cole ate next to nothing—like he had evolved from an air fern or something. Catherine knew it was a power struggle by her feelings of defeat and anger. When we looked at roles and responsibilities, Catherine agreed that it was her job to buy the groceries and to prepare nutritious meals at regular times, and that it really was Cole's job to do his own eating. After all, he could feed himself, so when he was hungry, he'd no doubt do it. That was his role and responsibility—not mom's job.

When she worries that her child is not eating enough, she is saying that she feels *she* knows better than her child about how much he should eat. When he doesn't, she takes over his job. She is not showing respect and faith in her child's ability to mange this job. She goes back and tries to *make* him eat! By micromanaging eating, the child loses his power to mom, and in an attempt to gain it back, he struggles and refuses to cooperate.

In each power struggle we must step back, take a deep breath, and have a look at the entire situation. We need to apprise ourselves as to what the real *needs of the situation* are. This is key in democratic families, because as social equals we are working to move away from using any one person's authority and instead honoring the laws of the social order. It is the reality of the situation that dictates what should happen next, not personal whims or wants. For example, children should go to bed at a set, routine time, one that is in keeping with the child's age and sleep requirements. Not when mom is simply fed up and deems them cranky. The reason they need to go to bed now is "because it's your bedtime" and not simply " because I said so." If a child does not like her bedtime, we don't fight nightly about it, hoping one person's way will beat out the other.

This means asking yourself: What really needs to happen in this situation? Is there a common logic that could be applied here, as opposed to my own logic? Yes, Jane does need to be clean and healthy, but must Jane have a bath tonight, at 7 p.m. sharp, like every night, because that's the way I prefer it done—after snack and before PJs? But wait a minute—why? Must it be at this time? Must it be every night? Maybe Jane is demanding to have more choices and more say, since this involves her!

> *Tugs of war are interpersonal and subjective, and they drag your* **relationship** *into the picture, making it a part of the issues at hand, and complicating the simplest of scenarios.*

When we are in a power struggle, we tend to put all our focus on the other person and what he is doing wrong and how he needs to change. This "other" focus is problematic because:

1. The other person perceives us as wanting him to change, and this feels manipulative and controlling to him. He will feel we are usurping his power, and this gives birth to his need to struggle and fight.
2. We feel a loss of our own control when we invest in outcomes that are predicated on OTHERS changing.

We truly can't control others, try as we may, nor is it our job to!

We need to refocus. We need to be concentrating on what the situation requires in a commonsense sort of way, and what OUR responsibilities and roles are, so we can decide what WE need to be doing to control ourselves ONLY. When we change our maneuvers to focus on ourselves, and thereby stop co-creating a fight, it necessitates a change in the other.

In the case of the purloined granola bars then, it is Janice's job and responsibility to have food in the house for healthy meals and lunches. It is not her job to police food consumption and storage.

When Janice goes into "lockdown mode," it's her private solution to the problem of controlling what her daughter should eat and when. Since Samantha was not invited to participate in the creation of the solution, she feels imposed on, which invites her thievery and sneaking to re-establish her rights.

Yet, people can't just eat whenever they want—that would be anarchy and chaos, and would violate the communal living laws. Janice's time and money in shopping and preparing food would be disrespected if systems of cooperation were not in place. So how can Janice and Samantha find the balance?

> *A child's power struggle is a clear cry that she would like MORE power and MORE SAY in this area of life.*

Janice needs to redefine her role—her responsibility is not to micromanage her daughter's snacking. Instead she needs to be thinking about how she can appropriately hand over more power to her daughter in the area of food choices and consumption rules.

GOOD MOTHERS ARE IN CONTROL

O—Offer Up an Olive Branch
The olive branch is a symbol of peace. This step in the process is about making gestures to show we are unwilling to fight. Here's how:

1. *Body language.* If your hands are on your hips, drop them to your sides. If your eyes are glaring harshly, soften your gaze. If your voice is terse, become quiet and gentle with your tone. If you're standing far apart, get closer. If you're towering above the child, drop to you knees, eye to eye. Rub her shoulder softly, or hold her hand gently while you talk. Your body language and words should reflect your intent NOT to fight and challenge. These gestures set the tone. They are 80 percent of your communication. Watch how your children will respond in kind. If you get harsh—they get harsher, if you get quiet and calm, they follow suit. WE must go first! You controlling mothers will love this because it will feel like your own little dimmer switch! You're actions and words can increase or decrease the conflict. Go ahead—get calm first and watch your child follow!

2. *Our words.* Our words become weapons in times of conflict—be sparse and choose them carefully. Consciously switch from talking to listening. Try some of the following lines:
   - "I'm not willing to fight about this." Say these words in a warm tone. But remember, it has to be your honest intention. If you really do want to fight and you say you don't, your children know your true intentions and will disregard your words. Have YOU decided not to fight?
   - "You're right—I can't make you. But would you be willing to help me out?" When we recognize and acknowledge the child's power in the situation this way it is often enough to end the struggle. Children

like to be helpful—they just don't like to be "made" to do things. You can help them to feel they don't need to be defensive by openly asking them to co-operate. You'll be surprised how effective this question can be.

3. *Listening.* Instead of yelling and lecturing—LISTEN! We want to understand their point of view and perspective on the issue at hand. We don't have to like it, but we do need to understand it. When children feel listened to and understood, they feel more aligned with you and often the power struggle ends.

4. *Humor.* You simply can't be laughing with someone and fighting with them at the same time! You may have already experienced the effectiveness of this when you tried to lighten a situation that was getting tense. Use this technique more. Make a conscious effort to lighten up yourself! "Hey, monkey girl—you looking for bananas up there? I see armpits I can tickle…"

> *We are more apt to be warm-hearted and humorous when we are not tired, run down, and frustrated. If you are getting in a lot of power struggles, you may want to reread Chapter 1, which deals with self-care, and start with attending to your own needs.*

Once we've offered the olive branch and changed to a more loving atmosphere where people don't feel they need to be guarded, we are able to think creatively about a *multitude* of ways that the problem could be solved—TOGETHER. The more children feel they have room for choices and a sense that they are involved in solution building, the more they will feel empowered, sense their equality, and be willing to cooperate.

Cooperation is a byproduct of feeling equal.

For example, Janice can inform Samantha that she is not willing to police the granola bars she buys for lunches. She can explain that she is willing to have treats in the house if her daughter is also willing to discuss when to eat them and how much to eat, in such a way that strikes a balance both can live with. She invites Samantha's input to find an outcome that is best for both instead of instigating a my-way/her-way approach that invites conflict and rebellion:

> How can we work something out together? It seems to me you would like to have more access to snacks. Is that right? You don't like my hiding them? My concern is this: I am worried that the supper I make will not be eaten, and I am also worried that there will be nothing left to put in your lunch pack if you eat the granola bars at other times. How can we solve these issues together in a way that works for us both?

Now Janice has put forth her true concerns instead of simply her own solution of "no granola bars."

Put forward your concerns and your desire for a solution, as opposed to your solution and the demand for compliance.

P—Push On Positively!
Once you have successfully offered the olive branch and established in your own mind what your roles and responsibilities are, you need to keep moving forward, with actions instead of words,

being firm and friendly at the same time. With each success you will grow more comfortable with the idea that the less control you attempt to wield, the more positive the outcome—not just for you, but for your entire family.

POWER: THE DIRTY WORD

Handing over control is often easier said than done, especially at first. Parents fear that they already can't control their children, and if they gave them more power, they would totally lose control. Most parents work to regain control of their children by applying even more control, which invites more rebellion, and so it goes in a spiral fashion leading to misery.

Yes, it is a leap of faith for some—especially those controller moms who have relied almost solely on control for their child guidance and who have inadvertently modeled the very manipulative and controlling behavior they find awful in their children. The entire family needs to move to a new model for sharing power amongst its members so they can stop the eternal spiral of fighting and get back to enjoying each other. You now have some methods you can use to get out of the power struggles you find yourself in today, now let's take a look at what you can do to empower your kids and avoid power struggles before they begin.

FAMILY MEETINGS: YOUR BEST PARENTING TOOL!

In order to have a democratic family, you must have a democratic process in place. Family meetings are the tools that democratic families use to get away from heated flare-ups and move toward calm group problem solving. Just as you have team meetings at work, so to do the members of your family need to meet to discuss how family life is going for everyone. This is where every member voices his or her concerns and is a part of the process of problem solving, conflict resolution, and establishing the arrangements the family lives by.

The value of holding family meetings can't be understated. This is *the* most powerful tool in moving your family towards egalitarian relationships, which are required if we are to hope for cooperation from our children.

THE HOW-TO'S OF RUNNING A FAMILY MEETING

I can't tell you how excited I am about teaching you about family meetings. If you can nail this parenting tool, you are set! You will create the conditions that will lead to the most significant changes in your family. The family meeting establishes your family as truly operating in a democratic fashion, and the benefits are immeasurable to your own happiness, to family cohesion, and to raising children who are cooperative problem solvers, well poised to reach true life fulfillment. Let me give you the nuts and bolts of how to pull these meetings off, because there are lots of niggly, technical details you'll need to know. I'll try to be as specific as I can to best ensure you can get off and sailing with these right away.

Creating a Safe Place to Speak Freely
There are few families that can open the floor to topics like these without the kids becoming so excited to share, and so excited to be listened to finally that they all start talking over one another, fighting to be heard. It's exciting to have a family meeting! They want to say their big ideas!

We want to keep that enthusiasm, but we need to do some initial training about how to respectfully share the floor. I suggest you try using a "talking stick."

> *A talking stick is used by Native Americans and First Nations people during their counsel circle to indicate whose turn it is to speak and to ensure they have both the freedom to speak without fear of interruption, and also the freedom to speak without fear of reprisal.*

In our house the talking stick was a saltshaker. We used this until people got the hang of listening without interrupting and taking turns speaking. Eventually the saltshaker was retired as everyone learned to do this without the reminder.

The most important element of the talking stick is that it helps us to work together to create an environment where people feel safe from criticism so that they can open up and communicate honestly.

Time

You need to hold these meetings once a week, and every week. Don't start skipping, moving them around, and rescheduling them, or you're going to run into trouble. They need to become a habit, a tradition, and a family expectation. Put it in your Outlook as a recurring task or write it on the family calendar as an appointment, and then delegate the task of reminding the family to one of the kids.

You also don't want these things to drag on like a bad funeral. Make them short and sweet and positive, starting at about 10 to 15 minutes initially.

Attendance

The expectation is that everyone in the family should attend the family meeting, including the little ones, even those who still can't speak. After all, you are calling together the family—and that means *everyone*. Grab the baby and nurse him, and have your little one pulled up in the highchair so she is in action, too. Offer a few quiet toys or toss them some crackers to nibble and stay busy with. For toddlers you can bring paper and crayons to the table. I don't want everyone distracted with activities, I'm just suggesting that you do what you need to do in order for everyone to gather, and to make it conducive for people to stay together for these brief discussions.

GOOD MOTHERS ARE IN CONTROL

It is important that you don't make attendance mandatory. Who likes being mandated to do anything? That would only serve to prove you have power over them, and that is exactly what we are trying to avoid here! Besides, a mandated attendee will work to sabotage your meeting. Instead, you can let that child know that he'll be missed, that you enjoy his company and input, and just be sure he is aware that any decisions made at the meetings apply to everyone in the house whether they are attending the meeting or not. If he would like to have his say and input, he needs to attend.

It's crucial that everyone has a voice—but let's remember, mom and dad, your voice is not to be louder or higher than the children's. Remember, this is about democracy. If your children moan and go limp on the floor at the mere mention of it being family meeting time, get the hint. Your children aren't going to come running to a meeting where mom lines everyone up to spout off about what the kids are doing wrong and to lay down the new rules of the week. It's not supposed to feel like being sent to the principal's office for heaven's sake. If the children don't feel empowered to make changes, or if the tone is always negative, no one will want to attend. Yourself included.

Format of the Family Meeting
I want you to shape your meetings to a format that your family enjoys. You should feel free to customize them so they become special family rituals for you. Let me give you some of the basics that you can build from or shape around.

Decide on someone to chair the meeting, and a secretary to keep minutes. In the beginning, mom and dad can take on these roles, but once your meetings are humming smoothly, you can all rotate. My kids started to chair the meetings at about the age of five, and as soon as they could write they were taking the minutes. They just eat this up! They love the ability to participate in such important ways and to be respected for their helpfulness.

I suggest you keep your meeting minutes in a book because you are going to want to refer back to them to see what was decided and what issues you are currently working on. And, can I just say, they make for great memorabilia too! I never did have time to sip tea in a rocking chair and journal about my mothering experiences—but we have the family meeting book and it's a treasure chest of memories. The kids even like looking back at it, laughing at their handwriting and seeing the things that were going on for them at that time. I still have some from my own childhood, too.

Here are the steps I suggest you include in each meeting:

1. *Appreciations*. You have to set the tone of positivity and you can do that by giving appreciations. This is so important that if you have no time for anything else on the agenda, have a meeting just to give appreciations weekly. They are medicine for the soul of the family. We don't appreciate each other and the family team anywhere near enough. Here are some ways to get the ball rolling.
   - "One thing I enjoyed about being in this family this week was …"
   - "One thing that someone did for me this week that I appreciated was …"
   - One thing our family does really well is …"
2. *Old business*. Of course, you won't have any "old business" at your initial meeting, but thereafter you will want to follow up on anything you tried to implement. This is a critical step not to be missed for two reasons:
   - Your children are going to be way more willing to try a solution if they know it will only be for one week. It's much easier to get buy-in and consensus if children know it's time-limited.
   - The family meeting is about problem solving, so we need to show children that there is a constant feedback loop of assessing, learning from mistakes, tweaking to

improve solutions, and coming up with the next best approximation of what we're trying to accomplish.

3. *New business.* Find a place to post the agenda for the family meeting so that anyone in the family can put items on the agenda that they would like to discuss as things come up throughout the week. Janice might say to her daughter, "Okay, I can see you're really not pleased with the granola bar solution I came up with, would you like to put snacks on the family meeting agenda and see if we can come up with something better?" Often that will stop a fight right in its tracks! When your children see you writing it down, it feels very affirming. They can see that they don't need to fight—but that they will have the opportunity to try to change things at the meetings.

A word of warning: keep the agenda fairly free of your own items initially. Wait until you feel you've got the positive tone and have established trust with the kids.

The chairperson reads the items on the agenda and whoever added it to the agenda now has the opportunity to talk about it. Here is where being the chairperson takes some skill. The focus must stay on identifying the current problem and making suggestions for solutions to try. It is not about rehashing the laundry-inspired argument of last Wednesday! The chairperson needs to watch for and cut short finger pointing, blaming, and recounts of past wrongdoings. It doesn't matter what transpired in the past—what we need is a suggestion for what to do in the FUTURE!

Once the problem has been stated (and hopefully not fought over yet again), you'll need to involve everyone in the brainstorming of new ideas. Let me say one more time for you control moms: EVERYONE comes up with ideas. This is about *mutual* problem solving, so you have to sit on your hands and hear the children's ideas. You might think their ideas are bizarre or unlikely to succeed. Well, it's not so much the quality of the decision per se, but the process of coming up with the solution that makes all the difference. Children are more likely to adhere to the decisions and rules that they helped establish.

You'll have many solutions to pick from, so you're going to have to narrow it down and decide on one idea—not the perfect or best idea, but simply one idea that everyone can agree to implement for one week only. You have to agree based on consensus.

> *Consensus*
> *1 have had my opportunity to sway the group to my way of thinking, and although 1 have been unsuccessful, 1 am willing to go along with the group in order to move things forward.*

Children need to learn that they always have a say—but they don't always get their way. You may have some who don't like the idea, but since you need consensus, you can acknowledge that they don't like it, and ask them if they'd be willing to go along with the group and try it for just a week. Most often, people who are asked to help the group will agree because they enjoy feeling socially interested and helpful.

4. *Review of people's activities in the week ahead.* Another great use for the family meeting is just to coordinate schedules and plans: Tommy needs to get to the mall to buy new soccer shoes before the big tournament on the

weekend—when can we do that? Pamela needs a ride to choir competition on Friday afternoon—is someone available to do that? Library books are due Thursday—how can we get those back on time? We're going to Grandma's on the weekend, people need to think about packing and things to take for the car ride.

Some families also use this time together for getting input into the family menu planning or assigning jobs around the house and similar family business. Frankly, I don't know how people could function without a family meeting!

5. *Closing.* I can give you a bit of a heads-up that some of your meetings will be filled with drama. It helps to get on with reconnecting after friction. Plan to wind up your meeting and then to do something fun together, like playing charades, a board game, or cards, or having a family video night with popcorn. This continues the theme of team building, an important component missing in many families today who rarely spend more than a few hours under the same roof together, let alone engaged in the same fun activity!

Still need convincing that family meetings are for you? Just look at the benefits to your children and family. In particular, family meetings can help your children develop important skills and qualities, such as these:

- Problem solving
- Conflict resolution
- Communication skills (both listening and expressing emotions)
- Empathy through learning to see another person's point of view on a situation

- Feeling empowered and encouraged that they can have a voice and a say in the family and that they *can* make a difference
- Feeling a sense of belonging and sense of equality with the others in the family
- Feeling a greater sense of ownership for the solutions to the problems and a greater willingness to live by the agreements cooperatively
- Greater willingness to help out others in the family and eventually the larger community (this replaces a "what is in it for me" attitude!)

Helpful Tips to Get You Off on a Good Start

I hope I have you all psyched up to start holding family meetings. You're probably ready to start tonight and to finally talk about that damn knapsack strewn all over the front foyer that you've been stepping over for the last few months.

I'm glad I've got you turned on to the idea, but I recommend you don't start with a big issue that's been going on for a while.

I am recommending that if you want these meetings to go well for you—take the slow approach. For your first month of meetings, simply open with appreciations and then have a single item on the agenda: for example, "What will we do for family fun this week?" What kid doesn't want to come to that meeting and solve *that* problem!

You still have to use all the same skills to address that problem as you do the knapsack issue—problem solving, brainstorming, and how to get to consensus, as well as practicing listening, taking turns talking, and feeling safe suggesting ideas. By talking about something fun, your children will learn about how family meetings operate and discover the meetings' usefulness, all in a positive way. After about a month, go ahead and add to the agenda some item the children would like to see improvements in, and a month or so later, you can try adding an agenda item for something you would like to see improved in the family.

Here are some items from my own family agendas over the years:

- Lucy—help with Halloween costume and how we'll decorate the house
- Zoe—getting a pet guinea pig (remember, everything is based on consensus!)
- Mom—toothpaste stuck to sink basin
- Dad—people interrupting when others are talking
- Lucy—wants to go back to that paint-your-own-pottery place
- Mom—wants to discuss the pens and pencils going missing from the kitchen
- Zoe—can we have another garage sale
- Dad—people leaving their socks laying about
- Mom—thermos left to mold in knapsacks
- Zoe—would like to take singing lessons
- Planning trip to aunt Dottie's 60th birthday party in Connecticut
- Lucy—privacy, people borrowing my things and going into my room without permission
- Zoe—writing on top of other people's work

You GOTTA try family meetings. Yes, it will take some repetition and time to get them established, but the benefits are too huge to miss out on. Put the effort in!

I promise you will learn just how powerful the family meeting is as a method to gain control over a situation rather than control over the children. Your kids will become cooperative as they feel their equality in the family is being recognized and honored. The whole family comes together as one solid team. This is the ticket for getting harmony back into a house laden with conflict.

Unless, of course, your children are too busy tied up in fisticuffs and bloody noses to even get to the family meeting. (I know all about this one—my brother once chased me with a pair of pliers above his head screaming bloody murder!) There is no worse conflict for a mother than that of her children physically fighting—so if your kids are going to battle every day with each other, read on: the next chapter will help.

CHAPTER 6

MYTH:
GOOD MOTHERS MANAGE SIBLING CONFLICT

GOOD MOTHERS MANAGE SIBLING CONFLICT

> *"I don't believe an accident of birth makes people sisters or brothers. It makes them siblings, gives them mutuality of parentage. Sisterhood and brotherhood is a condition people have to work at."*
>
> —Maya Angelou

What mother doesn't want her children to grow up to be great friends? After all, these are the people we will share the greatest amount of our life with, longer than our parents, our partners, and even our own children. Our siblings are an essential part of the reason we are the person we are today. We are cast in relation to them our whole lives long. It's an intense relationship that can either forge a special bond or drive a hurtful wedge between us.

The "good mother" ideal insists we manage our children's relationships, ensuring they do in fact love and care for one another—dammit! And boy, few things make us feel more like a failure than when they fight. So what are we supposed to do when Jamie starts kicking his sister simply because *her* leg is on *his* side of the couch? I can tell you that most modern-day good moms deal with this situation in pretty much the same way: "We do *not* kick in this family! Go to your room right now and don't come back until you are ready to say sorry to your sister."

Sound familiar? I'll betcha each and every one of us has said that exact line. Some of us said it a half dozen times this week alone! Unfortunately, it's the wrong thing to say and do.

Yes folks, 10 million good mothers CAN be wrong.

I can hear the breaks of your brains screeching to a halt—Whoooa!

Isn't putting them in a time-out and making them apologize what this whole positive and non-punitive parenting thing is all about? Isn't this the respectful alternative to administering a spanking?

Oh, come on! If we can't spank them, and we can't put them in a time-out—what's left? Do we just stand there while our children are pummeling each other? What kind of a mother would do that? Certainly not a good one!

The current societal myth dictates that the good mother *is* responsible for managing this situation. She must jump in and break up kids' fights, discipline the batterer, and console the wounded. After all, good mothers run the family. It's their domain, and they gotta make sure it's all running smoothly, interpersonal relationships included. Women are socialized from a very young age to pay attention to relationship matters. We go out of our way to make sure everyone is getting along. We watch more closely than our male counterparts for subtle signs and gestures of interpersonal stress and strain, like, say, the taking of a rubber T-ball bat to a brother's head, or the sudden appearance of dental imprints on a swollen arm. Ouch! Things can get really rough with siblings, and the pressure is on us moms to *make it stop*. Only peaceful children, please. Didn't you get the memo?

It doesn't help matters that society as a whole has changed its attitudes on children and fighting. After the murderous events in Taber, Alberta, and Littleton, Colorado, we now fear we could potentially be raising a monster child. If little Aiden snatches his sister's Barbie and pulls its head off gleefully, we worry about where this act of cruelty could lead.

It's stressful trying to raise children against the backdrop of the "War on Terror" and in the midst of nation-wide anti-bullying campaigns. Believe me, zero-tolerance attitudes abound and we good moms are the ones who are supposed to be the disciplinarians, making sure we have kids who comply. Now the jubilant three-year-old jumping around in his Spiderman pajamas and dealing karate kicks three inches from his brother's face just feels too violent.

While the pressure and fear on mothers is immense, I believe these are also signs that the time is ripe for society to learn the "how to's" of raising cooperative children. Learning the basics of how to get along in the face of diversity is a theme in our families, our communities, and between countries. Old notions of domination and supremacy have wreaked enough havoc in the form of racism. We no longer aspire to use power and domination to push one ideal. We want to learn to live together with our differences, be it between siblings, neighbors, or countries. We can help teach our children to get along by creating the conditions that foster it.

We need to come to grips with the notion that we moms do NOT hold power over our children and their affairs with each other. It's *their* relationship, and regardless of their age children are the caretakers of their relationships with each other. It's their "work," as Maya Angelou puts it—not ours. In fact, our interventions rob them of this duty and serve only to create distance and deepen a chasm between them.

In the pages ahead, I will show you why children fight and how our "good mother" interventions are not helpful. I will then offer you two effective means for dealing with fighting that will help your children get on with their work towards building wonderfully enriching brotherhoods and sisterhoods.

UNDERSTANDING WHY THE HECK KIDS FIGHT, ANYWAY

If we want to reduce fighting in our families, we first have to understand what fights are really all about. Let's dissect the dynamics of a fight.

As we have already learned, all behaviors serve a purpose, and one of our jobs is to figure out just what that heck that purpose is, exactly. Kids fight together because they both stand to get some positive result. No one actually likes the feeling of the fight itself. It's uncomfortable and stressful, so there must be some pretty enticing ancillary benefits that make the taking of a kick in the shin worth it.

Let's see if we can figure out the gains to be had for Yvette's two children, Tina (three) and Jonathan (six):

Yvette was busy peeling potatoes for supper while keeping an ear on the kids in the basement. It sounded like things were starting to get unpleasant down there, when suddenly there was a loud crash and then crying.

Yvette ran downstairs and found Tina bawling and holding her head, while Jonathan sat smugly with his arms crossed in front of him. Yvette scooped up Tina into her arms, kissed her hurt head, and hugged and comforted her.

"What did you do, Jonathan?"

"Nothing! She tried to grab my Transformer from me."

Tina, huddled in her mom's arms, points to her older brother and says, "He pushed me!"

Mom didn't see who had done what, but she knows how Jonathan can play rough and unfairly with his sister. His smug and cold attitude towards his hurt and crying sister make her think he is mean and unfeeling. She gets angry with him.

"Jonathan, come on, when are you going to give it up? I am sick of this! You're six years old—you should know better by now. You could have really hurt her. She's smaller than you and doesn't understand. Now go to your room and think about what you've done. Come back when you're ready to say you're sorry."

Seems everyone ended up unhappy! Tina's hurt, mom is angry, and Jonathan got punished. Who wants any of that?

Well, let's look again and see the hidden positive outcomes this fight procures for each.

Positive Results of Fighting for Baby Tina

At first glance, it looks like poor little Tina took a beating from her big ole mean brother who doesn't share well. But if we look closer, we see how Tina contributes to and benefits from fighting.

Tina, the baby of the family, really enjoys being babied, and especially pulling mother into her service to protect and coddle her. It makes her feel loved and special. Tina instigates fights expecting this motherly response. She pushes her brother's buttons knowing he will eventually snap and push or hit her so that she can cry and tattle. That makes mommy come snuggle her and offer protection from her brother. How special she must be to mother!

When Tina and Jonathan are fighting, they're in a power contest, too. Jonathan is older, bigger, and smarter, but wise little Tina can play her trump card and conquer her brother any time she pleases simply by screaming and crying. The baby has mom on her side, and she'll come rushing to Tina's defense, believing (mistakenly) that she's out-powered and incapable of managing her brother. Yvette acts as arbiter in their dispute and resolves their power struggle by finding Jonathan guilty of pushing and Tina is, once again, deemed the innocent victim. Jonathan is sentenced to time in his room.

Tina wins; Jonathan loses.

Tina isn't just fighting over who has the Transformer, no. She's fighting in a competition for status, to prove who is superior as they compete for mother's love. When mom embraces Tina and sides with her, even though she was complicit in the fight, she shows Tina favoritism and Tina wins!

Not stated, but implied: "Nana nana boo-boo—Mom loves me more than you!"

> "The biggest source of discouragement for a child is the feeling that a sibling is preferred."
>
> —Dr. Rudolph Dreikurs

The children know they BOTH had a hand in the fight. They do in every fight. It always takes two people to co-create a fight. But only Jonathan faces retribution, while the "victim's" involvement goes unrecognized and unpunished.

Moms are blind to just how so-called "victims" play an active part in the fighting, especially when they are very small. Don't be fooled. Hopefully, you'll start to recognize the baby's participation more readily now, even before the age of one year. In the case of the Transformer fight, here are some of the ways Tina participated in an active way to fight:

- Tina chooses to grab the Transformer because she knows it is his absolutely favorite and most verboten toy and the most likely toy to start a fight. She could have chosen a different toy. But no. She doesn't want a toy—she wants a fight.
- She could have let go of the Transformer herself when he started tugging to circumvent the fight—maybe asked for a turn or tried to barter. But no—she is trying to ignite a fight! She holds on tight and refuses to let go.
- She could run away or apologize when he gets upset, but she decides instead to stay in the line of fire. Who stands around waiting to get pushed? Someone who wants a fight.
- She could choose to play somewhere else in the house or with another sibling—but no, she chooses to stay and have conflict.

Benefits of Fighting for Bigger & Bossier Johathan
So what does Jonathan stand to benefit from fighting, then? It seems he is the one who gets treated unfairly and punished while the baby shines. What could that be the good of fighting like this for Jonathan? Let's see this fight from his perspective.

First, Jonathan had not meant to yank so hard that his sister would fall. That was an accident and they both knew it. Jonathan felt bad initially. He doesn't like to see his little sister hurt. But when he noticed she was screaming louder than needed, that she was crying hard to get him in trouble, he felt resentment. His genuine remorse and empathy disappeared when she called in her "re-enforcements" (a.k.a. mom).

When mom came to Tina's defense, mom just assumed Jonathan was in the wrong by asking the question "What did you do, Jonathan?" The presumption of guilt tells Jonathan what his mother thinks of him, and it's not very nice. Then, given the conflicting reports of what happened, mom chose to side with his sister's version, clearly showing favoritism to Tina, which hurts him deeply.

Jonathan feels like his sister makes his life hard. He is supposed to "know better," "set an example," and "yield to her" because she is younger. Jonathan feels it is unfair favoritism toward Tina whom he knows can manage on her own. Mom's repeated favoritism makes Jonathan resent Tina and feel hurt by mom.

At this point, their sibling relationship is headed for trouble. They are becoming rivals. He is losing interest in cooperating with his sister. He doesn't want to share with her, and is mad that he is made to. He pushes her as revenge for how she ruins his life. He figures he is gonna be the fall guy again anyways—may as well make it worth it!

With a sister like Tina, who is such a goody-two-shoes, how can he possibly compete and be as good as her? He figures if he can't be the "best at being good," he can always try his hand at being the "best at being bad." Jonathan begins to play the tyrant role in the family. If Tina's significance can come from being an incapable baby, he can get his sense of importance through being a powerful mean guy.

Once Jonathan has a belief about how life works in his family and his role in it, he sets about organizing life to unfold according to those rules. He actual sets up situations to prove he is less loved, and treated unfairly in situations so that he can say, "SEE! I knew it—life *is* unfair, there they go again siding with her! Look how I am always mistreated in this family!" When he refuses to share his toy, he knows he is setting up a situation of conflict that will prove his point yet again.

CYCLE OF DISCOURAGEMENT

All too often, our discouraged children get the worst treatment from us, when in truth they are the ones who need the most.

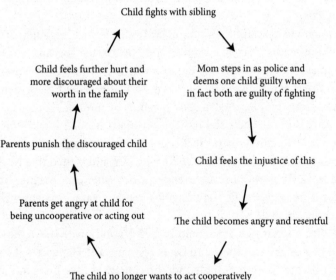

Child fights with sibling

Child feels further hurt and more discouraged about their worth in the family

Mom steps in as police and deems one child guilty when in fact both are guilty of fighting

Parents punish the discouraged child

Child feels the injustice of this

Parents get angry at child for being uncooperative or acting out

The child becomes angry and resentful

The child no longer wants to act cooperatively toward others in his family; feels discouraged and may act aggressively now

GOOD MOTHERS MANAGE SIBLING CONFLICT

MOM'S PERSPECTIVE

Mom wants to be a good mother and follow the societal norm of stepping in and taking matters into her own hands. But each mother, unaware of the dynamics of a fight, will view the situation through her own narrow and highly subjective lens, directly affected by the roles she played in her own family.

Baby

If mother was the baby in her own family growing up, she may well remember how awful it was to be picked on by older siblings and so she sympathizes with Tina. She might remember how she longed for her parents to do something about the bullying and so she tries to do better in her own family. It could also be that she remembers how she stirred up mischief and how truly capable she was as a child, and so she may not fall for the baby tricks in her own children. It is her own creative take, but it will influence how she deals with her own childern.

Eldest

What if mom was the eldest child in her family of origin? The eldest tends to be given a lot of responsibility and is expected to help look after younger siblings, set an example, and accommodate the others that are younger. The hassle and burden of this responsibility may mean that mom doesn't want to force that burden on her own children. She will be sensitive and more aware of this problem than mothers from a different birth order. Mom may feel badly *anytime* the eldest accommodates, so much so that she ends up giving favoritism to her own eldest instead. When we try to compensate and correct, we tend to go too far in the extreme and we must be mindful to find a middle ground.

Middle

Middle children tend to be the most discouraged in the family because they don't get the privileges of the eldest *or* the pampering of the baby. Middles have a hard time finding their place in the family, so they feel "squeezed out" and are much more likely to perceive favoritism and have issues with fairness. They feel they always get the brunt of the deal. Mothers who are middle children are usually very concerned with fairness in their own children. This is their issue. They feel compelled to stick up for the underdog. It's very hard for a middle-child mom to step out of her children's fights because of her tremendous need to make things fair. Unfortunately, by stepping in and trying to make things fair—she inadvertently creates more inequality!

> *If you were the bully in your family, you'll better appreciate where your bully's discouragement lies. If your personal experience was to* ***be*** *bullied, you will likely be convinced of your need to rescue.*

Yvette's involvement in managing her own children's conflict has provided benefits and payoffs that make their fighting worthwhile, and her supposedly helpful interventions are shortsighted and actually driving her children further apart. But there are other reasons for fighting too …

OH, THE MANY BENEFITS OF "DUKING IT OUT": HERE'S ANOTHER!

See if you can guess the benefit of fighting in this family:

Paul and Todd race to the table for lunch, both grabbing for the same chair. Mom, seeing the struggle, tells Paul to move over and give his brother the chair. Todd smirks at his victory. As the macaroni is served, Paul grabs the ketchup just to assure he gets *that* first, and sticks his tongue out at Todd, who then begins kicking Paul under the table. Mom tells them to stop it and eat. As a plate of cucumber slices is served, Paul takes as many as he can grab to hoard them from his brother. Todd complains to his mother and again she has to stop and deal with the misbehavior at hand. Mom can hardly get a bite of her own lunch down—she is so busy with the boys: "Put that down," "Give him one," "Stop that now," "Boys, that's enough!" She finds it all so tiring and it's over nothing, really!

Doesn't it sound like "thing one" and "thing two" have come for lunch? These two are like sparing partners, and they have an almost game-like attitude about their shenanigans. The boys go at each other constantly, but it never seems to escalate. Seems the only one really bothered by it all is mom. It *frustrates and annoys* her that she has to be on them all the time. These boys have learned to keep mother busy with them by stirring up sibling commotion and bickering. They have managed to make mother a captive audience, as it takes her full *attention* to be their peace-keeper. Mom feels obliged, because she feels peacekeeping is her "good mother" duty.

The benefit to their fighting is not about gaining favoritism, but simply gaining their mother's attention. Mom can remedy this situation by removing herself when they start with these kinds of acts. She can say, "call me when you two are calm," and with repetition, the boys will learn that if they would like to keep mother's company (and they do!), they had better learn to cooperate—otherwise she'll leave.

Are They Fighting for Your Attention?

*Clue #1—**Ask yourself: How are you feeling?***

- *Annoyed?*
- *Irritated?*
- *Frustrated?*
- *Worried?*

*Clue #2—**Ask yourself: What do you do when they fight? Do you nag, remind, and provide attention with little lines like these:***

- *"That's enough."*
- *"Come on, guys. Stop that right now!"*
- *"It's his turn now—you've had it long enough."*
- *"Play nicely, please."*
- *"Hey! Cut it out, you two."*
- *"I saw that …"*
- *"Stop that right now!"*
- *"We don't hit in this family."*
- *"We don't talk like that in this family."*
- *"Use your words."*
- *"Don't make me come over there!"*
- *"Gentle hands, please."*
- *"Inside voices, please."*

*Clue # 3—**What do your children DO in response to you?***

- *They stop momentarily, only to resume again a moment later.*

WHAT MOMS CAN DO INSTEAD: SOLUTION TIME

Yes—it's time to do things differently. It's clear that the current parental interventions and methods for dealing with sibling conflict actually create the *benefits* of fighting.

Moms can help their children build their relationships and re-duce the fighting between them by creating the conditions most conducive to the kids' *wanting to be cooperative.*

Cooperation only exists between social equals. In order to help level the playing field, moms can:

1. Reduce competition of all kinds in the family.
2. Stay out of the fights so the kids derive no benefit from fighting behaviors.
3. Recognize the cooperative nature of fighting—"put them in the same boat."
4. Invite children to put any issues they can't solve by them-selves on the agenda for the weekly family meeting.
5. Encourage, encourage, encourage!

REDUCING SIBLING COMPETITION

A staggering 85 percent of siblings feel that their parents show fa-voritism to one child. It is the favoritism that hurts, discourages, and creates ill will between children.

In a non-competitive family with no favoritism, fighting really is inconsequential because children don't need to fight to establish winners and losers in order to determine which sibling is superior over the other.

Fighting is not needed among those who feel as equals and are not concerned with the elevating or demoting of their status. So ask yourself, is your family truly non-competitive?

Ways to Reduce Sibling Competition

1. *Don't compare your children: "Tommy, why can't you keep a nice neat room like your brother Toby?"*
2. *Don't pit children against each other: "Fastest one to get ready and in the car wins."*

3. *Look for and foster each child's unique abilities and talents.*

4. *Don't label children (e.g., "my scholar," "the family athlete")
    because it pressures each child to be the "best" at something
    and leads the others to **not** participate in areas of interest that
    their siblings have dominated and succeeded in.*

5. *Don't be overly concerned with making things "fair." Trying
    to make things "equal" and "fair" between siblings is not only
    a losing proposition—it's misguided. **Equal and fair are com-
    petitive notions**. They assume your needs are related to what
    another has, and call attention to measuring and compar-
    ing again! When children complain, "He got more cake than
    me!"—instead of trying to even up the cake serving exactly,
    simply reply, "you don't need to worry about your brother. The
    question is, do you have enough cake for you?"*

6. *Drop the idea of "my big boy." If we get excited about being
    "big" or use diminutive terms for younger children, it gives the
    idea that big is better than small, and so younger siblings com-
    paring themselves will feel inferior. We want to notice and give
    importance to what people DO to contribute and be helpful,
    not what they are (e.g., big, pretty, smart).*

7. *Be sure to encourage instead of praise by commenting on the
    child's efforts and improvements instead of on perfection and
    end results: "You made your bed perfectly this morning!" is
    discouraging to a younger sibling who doesn't yet have the
    skill, but "you worked so hard to get your bed all made up this
    morning" can be said to any child of any ability.*

8. *Watch yourself and your partner as quiet competitors. You
    two set the mood of the household. Do you engage in power
    struggles with a win/lose formula with your spouse?*

There is no better way to instill or restore social equality between your children and in the family than placing the job of getting along back in the hands of the children. You will see immediate shifts in your children's behavior as you stay firm in your resolution to stay out of their fights.

STAY OUT OF THEIR FIGHTS!

Instead of mom feeling like she needs to be the family peacekeeper, managing her children's conflicts and elevating herself to a position of authority, she can simply STEP OUT.

That's right—ignore the fighting.

She can hand back to the children the responsibility of managing their own affairs. She can let them know that she has faith in them to work things out between themselves, and then simply walk away. She is not being negligent; she is being respectful of who truly owns the problem. She is showing trust and faith. She is refusing to give payoffs to their antics.

Let's walk through this scenario so we can see how mom's decision to step out and not get involved changes things for the better.

Yvette's Story—Take Two!

Mom, peeling potatoes for supper, hears Tina's cry. This time, mom is going to try something different. Mom is NOT going to respond. That's right. She stays put and keeps peeling potatoes. Yvette hears that Tina is really crying and probably got a bit hurt, but she can also tell that it is not a medical emergency.

Tina will wait, expecting her mother to fly in to save her. Failing her arrival, Tina will make her way upstairs to the kitchen with tear-streaked cheeks to report the crime: "He pushed me!"

Tina will be shocked when her mother replies, "Here's a hug, I am sorry you got hurt. I am sure you and your brother can work this out." And then mom can get back to her job of peeling potatoes.

"*WHAAAAAT*?" thinks Tina. No longer is she getting rescued. Being a little helpless victim doesn't impress mom anymore. It's not getting her the importance she seeks. Mom doesn't seem to be paying attention to her inabilities and baby-like qualities. Tina does like that mom has faith in her, though. That felt good to hear. Maybe Tina will have to think of other qualities to be important. Maybe acting "helpless" is not gonna cut it anymore.

Jonathan also waits for mom to come mistreat him again— but she doesn't! Hey! Jonathan, who has been so discouraged, thinks that maybe mom can see that Tina is not so innocent anymore. Jonathan no longer feels picked on and treated unfairly by his mom. He thinks maybe mom doesn't see him as such a bad boy anymore, that maybe he could try wearing a different hat in the family. It would be different to share his Transformer with Tina if nobody told him he *had* to. Besides, he likes giving her this act of kindness, and she knows he didn't have to share it, so she feels loved too!

Four fights later, when the children are starting to see that mom has indeed decided to stay out of their fights, Tina sees a perfect opportunity to knock down the fort her brother built. Tina thinks now: "Gee, if I do that, he could wallop me one—why bother? I don't want to get hit if Mom isn't going to do anything about it; I better not." Jonathan, feeling good about himself and his sister, asks, "Do you wanna see the neat fort I built? Come on inside!"

Tina and Jonathan are learning from each other all about the fine art of give-and-take, acquiescing, and adaptation that will make them cooperative human beings in all their future relationships.

GOOD MOTHERS MANAGE SIBLING CONFLICT

This learning to deal with one another and finding non-conflicting ways of resolving issues happens pretty quickly. In fact, it can happen in just a few hours, as I discovered when I was asked to babysit the kids of friends.

The older sibling was a girl (eight years old) who had long hair that she wore in braids. An hour into our time together, I heard her shriek. Her six-year-old brother was pulling on one of her braids. She looked to me to rescue her from this attack. She made no effort to defend herself. Her eyes were on me the whole time. I also noticed that he wasn't pulling her hair very hard. He had the opportunity to really yank, so why wasn't he? Why hold back? If he wants to hurt her—get on with it! The girl was two years his senior, bigger, and stronger—why didn't she fight back? Why does she do nothing except cry for an outsider's help to solve her problems?

As I was assessing the scenario, the behaviors, and the choices the children were making, I held in my mind the knowledge that it takes two to create a conflict. I knew my involvement, if not carefully planned, had the potential to make things worse.

So I reminded myself that this was what these two had decided to do together, and I simply said, "I am sorry you are having trouble with your brother, I trust you two can work it out together." I walked away. I don't know what happened after that, but when I returned later, everyone was playing, so I guess they figured something out.

This hair pulling happened twice more that afternoon, and each time I left, making a small comment like "that's not very fun for me to watch."

Out of the corner of my eye, I saw the young girl who was playing the role of the innocent victim waving her braids into her brother's face, taunting him with her hair, bugging him by swinging it in his face so he couldn't see. She was not the innocent bystander one would assume on first glance. After my refusing to become involved three times, the hair pulling stopped for the rest of the weekend.

I didn't need to teach them to cooperate, I simply eliminated the usefulness of the discord by not playing my part.

TRICKS OF THE TRADE: PUT THEM IN THE SAME BOAT

Since we now understand that sibling fighting is an act of collaboration between two willing parties, and that siding with one over the other creates resentment, competition, favoritism, and all things evil, let's look at a technique called "putting them in the same boat."

Caroline (14) and Emily (10) have been fighting over whose turn it is on the computer. Emily is angry that Caroline is always IM-ing with her friends, and won't ever give her a turn. The family room is always being disturbed by their fighting and constant harassments in the form of "Get off," "It's my turn," and "Jesse's online now, he's never on, let me on for just one minute—PLEASE!—oh, come on—God—I HATE YOU! Like one little minute is gonna make such a difference to you and your boneheaded friends."

Mom uses the technique of "putting them in the same boat." The metaphor paints the picture beautifully: each child's actions affect the other, like sharing a canoe. If you've worked together to paddle yourselves UP the creek, you're going to have to work together to paddle back down. It honors that both parties are culpable, that both got themselves into this mess, and both are responsible for getting each other out. They are bound together; the actions of one affect both. It really creates a situation where cooperation is necessitated instead of avoided.

Mom lets the girls know that if they continue fighting over the computer, it will be turned off and *neither* will have access. This is not a punishment. This honors the idea that with every freedom comes responsibility. If they would like the freedom of using the computer, they also need to accept responsibility for using it cooperatively and in a non-disturbing fashion. They both will have to face the same logical consequence of no computer access. Instead of mom feeling it is her motherly duty to resolve her girls' fight, mom can relinquish the job of finding an equitable solution for the girls. Mom can't be accused of taking sides and showing favoritism if she's not involved. Mom asks the girls to come up with their own solution for the problem of sharing the computer—one that that they can both agree on. Until they can agree on something, the computer stays off. Both are motivated to find a solution and no one is upset with mother.

If one child provokes the other, they both lose the computer. Hmm, now they're thinking twice before starting a fight! They are once again on a level playing field. Both hold the power to getting on and off the computer, and they are BOTH invested in getting along. The solution also takes the two of them to cooperate.

Matt and Dylan are both going fisticuffs in the family room. Mom can see it's getting very physical and so she decides to intervene. She can do this without taking sides by putting them in the same boat: "Boys—your fighting is disturbing everyone else's peace in the house. If you want to fight, take it outside." And then mom can show them the door.

Fighting without an audience loses a significant benefit. Most children will end their fight before they hit the screen door. This request that they fight outside is a powerful reminder that you are not getting into their fights. In a sense, you are honoring that you are powerless to make them stop. Two people who want to fight are going to fight! Ain't nobody gonna stop them. Honest. They have to decide for themselves when they have had enough.

The important point is that mom is able to view the fight as a combined effort, and she treats them as a pair. She could also "put them in the same boat" by asking them both to go to their own rooms to "cool down" or have a "time-out." So long as both befall the same outcome, you're going to be successful!

But They'll Get Hurt!

I know, I know. You really want to try walking away or asking them to go outside to fight, but you just don't trust them to not kill one another!

Well, brace yourself. In the short term, the fights are going to get worse. Why? Because when children no longer receive the payoff they were anticipating, they will redouble their efforts. Fighting will intensify as they attempt to work harder to draw you back in. When your children come to realize that NO AMOUNT of fighting is going to get you involved, they will eventually (quickly) give it up.

Remind yourself:

- If they really truly wanted to hurt each other, they would wait for some moment when no one could come to the rescue, not when you are sure to!
- Think of how many siblings there are across the country. If they wanted to hurt each other, every hospital emergency room would be lined up with kids! That's not the case. Ask any ER doctor. Kids' fighting is not how children end up in emergency.
- The best risk analysts are insurance companies, who rely on actuaries. If having a sibling was a health threat, there would be a premium you'd have to pay on your policy!
- When a brother or sister does misjudge and accidentally hurt a sibling, you can see the shock and concern immediately.

The BIG Mistake We All Make

I have to forewarn you about the one BIGGY mistake that mothers make in their attempts to ignore their children's fighting. They start out all excited to try a new tactic. They tell themselves they are no longer going to get involved in the fights, and then—BOOM—one erupts. They start off feeling proud, knowing all this good "psycho-dynamic" stuff, and having pledged not to give payoffs and make their fighting beneficial.

But then Mikey gets Jamie in a stranglehold...

Mom can't take it anymore! Mom feels she just *has* to step in now, so she loses her resolve to be strong and stay out, and instead she goes back to her old ways and breaks up the fight, dishing out lectures and punishment. When mom does this, she is inadvertently training her kids that mom ignores the little stuff—but not the big, intense fighting. If you want to get mom's involvement, you need to fight *really* hard. Oops—these actions have escalated the very conflict you were trying to diminish.

Move your game piece back to GO! Do not collect $200.

If you were really uninvested in your children's fight and ignoring it, you would never have seen the stranglehold in the first place. The kids need to feel your absence. Leave the house if you must—or take a good book to the bathroom and hang out in there with the door closed and locked. Let them know you'll be back out when the fight is over. Plug in your MP3 player to drown out the noise. When was the last time you got to sit and read, anyway?

> *If you are truly concerned about the violence—trust your gut instincts. Overly violent reactions and behaviors are a matter for counseling.*

Tip: *If you see a truck about to be bonked over a head, swiftly remove the truck without saying a word. Just know that if you weren't there at all, the truck would not have been lifted over the head in the first place!*

Put It on the Agenda

Often moms don't have faith that the children will come to a solution on their own. They fear one child will railroad the other into always getting his way. Any issue that the children can't solve on their own can be put on the agenda for the next family meeting and then the entire family can problem-solve the issue together. Often by the time the weekly meeting arrives, the issue has been resolved! You'll find that if you try to problem-solve with them during the fight, they are already too invested in seeking a win/lose outcome that they can't even entertain possible solutions. They just want to WIN. If we only problem-solve issues at family meetings when people are calm and feeling positive, the focus moves away from the personal and becomes focused on the issue instead. You are more likely to have real resolutions and solutions.

In acting as Good Mom, the police officer, peacemaker, and arbiter to your children's fights you inadvertently:

- *elevate your authority and thereby erode the social equality needed for cooperation in a democratic family,*
- *rob the children of owning their own problems and learning how to solve them,*
- *create favoritism and stimulate competition,*
- *deny them an opportunity to actually learn what it takes to*

get along with another person who has divergent wishes and wants,

- *heighten the drama by being an audience.*

However, if you step back and refuse to be involved in their fights, your children will:
- *learn creative ways to deal with one another and become problem solvers,*
- *learn the fine art of cooperation with its give-and-take,*
- *develop a sense of care and concern for their siblings,*
- *feel loving warmth and acceptance in the family, and*
- *take ownership for their relationship with their siblings.*

After all, kids need to learn how to be cooperative at home because the next stop is school! The very latest research has shown that cooperative children actually do better academically than competitive ones. Interesting, eh? Read on to see what mythical ideas we need to bust when it comes to the contentious issue of good moms "ensuring" good educations for their children.

CHAPTER 7

MYTH:

ONLY THE BEST EDUCATION FOR MY CHILD

ONLY THE BEST EDUCATION FOR MY CHILD

I t seems that as soon as you've got a grip on nursing and diaper rash, you have to start thinking, nay—worrying—about your child's education. You hear the other moms at drop-in who have already taken the plunge: "I love Luke's nursery school, but I'm starting to think maybe he's ready for more of a challenge. He's bored of gluing macaroni on a paper plate, he already knows his whole alphabet and is starting to read for Pete's sake!"

ALPHABET! Reading! Oh boy ... now the worry explodes as you think to yourself, "Oh my gosh—my Clare can't do that yet. Was I supposed to teach her that? Am I bad mother? I don't want her falling behind and thinking she isn't smart. I better get her caught up."

Caught up? My dear, where have you been? You are already way behind! Didn't you do fetal stimulation for brain development like the rest of us did? Oh, you should have. It's supposed to increase IQ, you know! Especially Mozart.

Hmm—is it true? Or hokey? What do you think? Are you going to risk being wrong and have your child forever in a trail of dust left by the others who got the Mozart advantage? Aren't we supposed to do anything we can to advance our children's development, and to help them reach their potential, even if that means plugging headphones into your belly? What the hell—can't hurt, eh?

This is a "fast" parenting culture, folks, and we are nothing short of obsessed. We feel we're the active agent in rearing a child well poised to succeed at the head of the pack, and these days that is synonymous with raising SMART children. Academic success is amongst our greatest ambitions for our children. It's the "good mother" credo. And if other moms are giving their kids academic steroids to win the race, so will we—even if we don't agree in principle.

Oh so sad, but true.

Let's explore the culture of educational enrichment and the per-vasive message mothers are being sent that spurs their involvement in this movement. I'll share the concerns mothers have about NOT jumping on the bandwagon, and show you how early enrichment and academic competition can backfire on well-intentioned moms and actually de-motivate your children from learning. I'll also of-fer up some do's and don'ts, so moms can find their suitable role in supporting their child's learning.

LIVING IN THE SMARTER-FASTER-SOONER CULTURE:

You just can't help but get swept away with it all when you live in a culture that is having a love affair with "enrichment". Smarter-Faster-Sooner is in vogue and it feels like the bus is leaving whether you climb on board or not. Mothers will open their wallets and pay richly for anything that promises to help their child get ahead, and marketers are only too happy to service this large and ever growing market segment.

"Educational" baby videos, such as "Baby Einstein," gener-ate over a hundred million dollars in profits every year. Disney just got in on the action, launching the new parenting magazine *Wondertime*, which offers moms practical methods of teaching and educating children—from newborn through to starting school. There is no shortage of literature on the how-to's, as the parent-ing section of bookstores are lined with book titles such as *How to Have a Smarter Baby*, *Smart-Wiring Your Baby's Brain*, *How to Raise a Brighter Child*, and *Baby Minds: Brain Building Games Your Baby Will Love*.

Sylvan Learning, Kaplan, and Kumon Learning Centers are popping up like convenience stores in every corner strip mall. It's a boom industry showing strong and steady increases in revenue every year. Educational supply stores like Scholars Choice have opened their doors to an eager public of moms who want to outfit their homes like little nursery schools.

God forbid you don't have the economic means—go in debt if you have to. This is critical stuff.

SCHOOLING AND EDUCATION ARE BAD? NOT TRUE!

I don't want you thinking that I am suggesting we go back to abacuses and trying to live the simple life of the Amish. I am actually on fire with excitement about the future for our children and education. I think BIG changes are on the horizon. Research, technology, and business are coming together to help our children learn outside the box. I think the whole process of education is about to change dramatically, including how and what we spend time teaching our children. We're thinking differently about information, given the new accessibility to it, and this will alter how we have done many things conventionally—including educating our children to be prepared to enter a wireless, on-demand world.

My beef is with the painfully slow death of the old conventions. Our current system of education is a dinosaur, created when we were training the masses to move away from agriculture and enter into the manufacturing-based labor force of the Industrial Revolution. Sitting in rows and doing rote drill learning is great practice for working the line and taking orders from above.

We are now schooling our children in the global economy of the Information Age, and knowledge drives our new GNP. The rigorous educational standards and formidable labor pool found in countries such as India and Japan are perceived as a threat. Jobs and whole industries are being moved offshore. All of these factors have combined to create the current frenzy in education, which feels reminiscent of the moon race. Goodbye phys ed., arts, and music; hello worksheets, homework, and drills.

Bottom line—our school systems are still largely autocratic, pedantic, and highly competitive by design, and we're throwing fuel on the fire by becoming MORE autocratic, more restrictive, more competitive, and more pedantic.

We could talk educational reform at length, but we have our children in schools NOW, and we want them to do well in the current system. How do we go about doing that? Our common parenting approaches actually hinder the learning process or come with secondary or long-term costs we are unaware of. So let's bust the common beliefs that good mothers have about securing the best education for their children, and offer an alternative viewpoint.

THE MYTHS THAT DRIVE GOOD MOMS TO WANNA "PUSH"

School is important for children. It's their first experience of society outside of and independent from the family. Yes, it's a place where they learn factoids, like what the Plains Indians ate and how beavers build dams, but to a personality theorist and mental-health professional, school is children's preparatory ground for the attitudes they will develop toward working, authority, and rules.

School is where children learn about living in groups with peers; they experience the give-and-take of sharing the classroom with 25 or 30 other children, and no longer having the benefit of constant individual attention. School is also the place children learn to handle ever-growing responsibilities and to build the skill set to manage and learn self-sufficiently.

These are all developmental process that happen in the background while academic learning fills the foreground. I think the background learning is the far more important of the two.

Learning itself is a natural process. If children are interested and intrigued and if they stay encouraged—I promise they will learn. The trick is to find that sweet spot where they are not bored because the work is too easy, nor giving up because the challenge is beyond them. We must honor the idea that each child has his or her own growing edge, and that edge is where the best learning happens. Who cares where that is compared to others?

I tell this to good mothers who are like a terrier on a bone with their kids' educational success, and even though my advice to them is to back off, stand down, let it go, have faith ... there is just no way these moms are going to let up for a moment. They feel the stakes are just too high and that it's their duty to assure that their children get the best education, even if that means anything and everything short of writing their children's essays for them.

These are well-intentioned moms who want to do well by their kids. They are operating under the influence of three myths, and if you believed these myths, you'd be a "push" parent too. These myths are:

1. I believe that if my child starts ahead, she'll stay ahead.
2. I believe the world IS competitive; if I don't raise a competitive child, he'll be overtaken by those who are.
3. I believe that without my involvement my child wouldn't achieve.

Let's look at each of these in detail.

A "GOOD" HEAD START

We have made terrific advances in understanding the brain and its development. It's the application of some of this learning that has me concerned. If a study of only 120 infants finds that early exposure to black-and-white geometric patterns increases neuronal activity in the visual cortex, does that mean we *all* must strip down the Beatrix Potter wallpaper in the nursery and paint it black-and-white checkerboard? And if the next study shows the enrichment possibilities of floral-patterned wallpaper, do we start ripping again?

It seems to be an unchallenged idea that "sooner is always better." This is a dangerous trend, because there is world of difference between presenting opportunities that encourage our children to be on their own distinct learning edge, and pushing for "timely conquest" over their inabilities. Competitive pushing of that sort sends the message that they are currently deficient and "less than" what they should be.

Interestingly, research has shown that in early learning there is a leveling effect over time. Nearly all early advances disappear as "advanced" children stabilize and "slower" children catch up. This is because the brain develops in a nonlinear fashion. Certain areas can be in a growth spurt while others are dormant, waiting their time. In the end, regardless of onset or duration, and failing neurological damages, our children will continue their maturational process and all eventually learn to speak, walk, use the potty, learn the alphabet, read, do addition, and all kinds of wondrous things that humans learn to do in their lifetime!

Parents are often unaware of the healthy and normal ranges for most of these processes. Take reading, for example. We're now told to have our children reading in kindergarten. However, if your child is at the tail end of the normal distribution curve, he may not become a reader until the end of the second grade. That is still within the range of developmental norms.

> Daniela enrolled her son Nathan in a preschool that has a great reputation for their academic excellence. As part of their early literacy program, Daniela has been asked to read an assigned book with Nathan. It comes home in a little plastic bag. Trouble is, Nathan won't sit still and do even this little bit of homework. He jumps down, interrupts, and takes no interest. Daniela is worried because he is still being sent home with the books from the lowest level.

There is no reason to believe that Nathan won't be a reader some day. Children will learn to read when the brain is developmentally ready. The best way to encourage reading is to be a reader yourself, to enjoy books with your children, and to keep the experience positive and exciting. We must have faith in the human developmental process. Unfortunately, like so many good mothers, Daniela is worried as a result of expectations that schools have pushed more aggressively, earlier and earlier. Unchecked, this fear causes her to become more pressured about reading.

> *"Don't let your schooling get in the way of a good education."*
> —*Mark Twain*

Nathan is none too happy either. Why can't he get this? He's knows full well the other children are reading in levels ahead of him. He knows his mom is not happy with him, and that he is disappointing her. Nathan is in a critical time of developing his self-concept as a learner. If this early pressure to learn material that he's unready to master leads him to develop a negative attitude towards learning or to think of himself as a "stupid" person, all future learning is in jeopardy. Believe me, it will be much harder to change his beliefs about himself as a student than it is to teach him his ABCs and 123s a year later. This is the very real risk behind the supposed advantages of pushing and pressuring children to accelerate their learning competitively.

Books with mom used to be Nathan's favorite time of the day, but the mandating of reading and mom's drilling to guess the letters has added pressure and judgment, which has robbed him of all the joy of books. He evades the task now, trying to squirm off her lap and do something else to get away from the situation. Daniela had intended to stimulate Nathan's interest in reading, but because of the pushing and pressuring, Nathan is now feeling that being a non-reader is an inadequacy that makes him inferior. Whenever he reads with mom, he feels this inferiority is being exposed, so he decides it is better to avoid the task altogether. When learning to read starts feeling like a competition he can't win, he ceases trying and drops out of the race.

This is the death of the learning process.

THE WORLD **IS** COMPETITIVE: IF I DON'T RAISE A COMPETITIVE CHILD, HE'LL BE OVERTAKEN

I swear, a week doesn't go by that I don't have to bust this myth. There is a general misunderstanding about that word "competitive." Parents assume that a child must be competitive, or else those kids who *are* competitive will outperform them.

The non-competitive child is actually *better* poised to excel at anything, including academics.

Let's define the "competitive child." This is the kid who feels that he MUST win. He has the mistaken belief that he must *be* the best, as opposed to *do* his best. He spends his time and energy concentrating on himself and how he's doing, instead of on the task at hand.

If you're a competitive person, believe me, you are not okay with failure and mistakes—you're too worried about your own need to be the best. After all, you've made the mistake of tying your personal worth to it. Now you're looking only for those things in life that you do well and can beat others in. We can't be best at everything, so that immediately limits your choices. You end up going after only those things you have fast and immediate success in. Those things may not even be of interest to you, but you excel so you feel safe and pursue them farther. You also stop pursuing anything in which you risk mistakes, failure, and looking bad.

You wake up at 40 as a charted accountant because math came easily to you, but is it what you wanted from life? If you felt like a loser in gym class, did you give up? Did you forfeit the lifelong joy of your favorite recreational sport? One comment about "throwing like a girl" and you were out of all athletics forever—such a shame!

Being competitive is a burden. It shuts us down and is an albatross we wear around our necks. If we truly want people to soar, then we must give them the courage to be able to make mistakes, face failure, learn, grow, and chase their dreams. The ONLY way to go from novice to mastery is through mistakes. The more comfortable you are with that process, the more likely you'll be to tackle the challenges of school.

Stop and think about it for a moment—what would you be doing right now if you didn't have to worry about looking bad and failing? Imagine having no concerns about looking foolish. No worries about what others would say or think of you. Imagine the unbelievable freedom and energy you could put into learning a task! Perhaps if you weren't competitive yourself you wouldn't worry about your child's schooling so much.

> "The competitive child must compete and win, whereas the encouraged child can compete whether he wins or loses."
> —Dr. Rudolph Dreikurs

Non-competitive children can compete, and they are not hindered with baggage and fraught with worry about making mistakes. In fact, you have to be courageous enough to make *many* mistakes and face *many* failures if you are to go on and achieve truly great things.

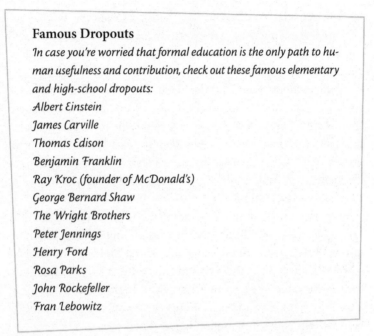

Famous Dropouts

In case you're worried that formal education is the only path to human usefulness and contribution, check out these famous elementary and high-school dropouts:

Albert Einstein

James Carville

Thomas Edison

Benjamin Franklin

Ray Kroc (founder of McDonald's)

George Bernard Shaw

The Wright Brothers

Peter Jennings

Henry Ford

Rosa Parks

John Rockefeller

Fran Lebowitz

WITHOUT MY INVOLVEMENT MY CHILD WOULD PERFORM BELOW POTENTIAL

Many moms believe they have to sit on their children if they want them to learn and do well at school; they worry that left on their own, their children would be happy getting a B. First of all, call me crazy, but what's wrong with a B, anyway? It means *average*, it means that your child is in fact performing at the expected level.

But average doesn't cut it any more, does it? Moms all want their children to be straight-A students, in every subject. Yet if they were, the schools would just move the bell curve and expectations up. We can't all be "above average" now, can we? It's a statistical impossibility. With the straight-A expectation planted in every single person's mind, the majority of students feel they're short of the mark when they are just fine! It's discouraging!

We've seen how the encouraged, non-competitive child excels, and how discouragement stops our kids short. When mothers get invested in their children's work and performance, they think they're helping but, in fact, they can be inadvertently very discouraging to their children, and this has costs.

Top Five Ways Our Involvement Discourages

1. *Loss of sense of ownership, pride, and satisfaction for their own mastery.* Tina enjoys helping eight-year-old Norah with her homework. She feels she is being a good, involved mother and is living up to the school's code of working collaboratively to help her child succeed. Tina checks Norah's creative writing assignment about their family's summer holiday. Not only does Tina proofread the assignment, correcting the sentences that have missing capitals or periods, she also suggests that Norah could improve her story by adding a section that has a map of the place they went, and a another page called "About the Author." Tina is really getting into the project and in a flash of brilliance, Tina suggests they could use her scrapbooking kit to cut up family photos and paste them on the cover with some glue to make it look like the beach they stayed at! When Norah gets her assignment back, she gets an A. While she is pleased to do well, she feels no sense of satisfaction about the job she has done. It feels like it was mom's project and the pride of succeeding after hard work is no longer there. To work and not derive satisfaction is demotivating. The assignment gets stuffed in a drawer.

2. *Your child may experience increased anxiety.* Benjamin knows he is smart and a scholar and that his parents are very proud of him. Mom never has to fight with Benjamin to do his homework. He is very responsible.

But Benjamin has been chewing his nails and gets severe stomachaches on test days. It seems to be getting worse each year. While Benjamin is excelling as his parents wish, he is always anxious about maybe not doing well in the future. He feels he is only as good as his last report card. Until the marks are in, he is anxiety-ridden and uncomfortable.

3. *Your child may feel like she's never good enough.* Petra worked so hard to get caught up in math. When she got a 16/20 on her test, she was really pleased with herself, but when she brought her test home for her parents to sign, her parents wanted to know why she missed the other four questions. It seemed that it was never good enough for her parents. Instead of celebrating her hard work and improvement, the focus was always put on her shortcomings. Petra was not motivated to try harder— she felt defeated by the notion that she was just never going to be good enough for her parents, so she stopped pushing herself at school. It wasn't worth it.

4. *Your child may feel that he can't be the social equal of his classmates.* When we create competitive schools, we pit child against child. Whatever happened to caring classrooms with students feeling a sense of citizenry? We keep asking children to be cooperative in the classroom, but then we create competition through countless activities, such as *student-of-the-week* awards and posting test results in rank order. This means that our students are not learning how to work cooperatively or how to enjoy the fruits of community. There are lots of smart people it the world, but companies will tell you that what is hard to find is someone who can get along with people! Seems that cooperation is more valued than letter grades in the workforce at the moment.

5. *Your child may rebel.* Tim's parents are in his face about school all the time. He has had it. He has decided to rebel. He has engaged in a power struggle with his mom who gets on him to get his homework done. At first, he tried to defeat her by simply lying about having finished his homework, and by hiding his assignments. The more he tried to be covert, the more interest she showed. She began looking through his bag for his work, and taking it upon herself to check the teacher's website for the assignments and test dates. Seems Tim couldn't work around his mom anymore, but rather than being defeated, he played the trump card. She might know when all of his work was due, but she couldn't actually make him learn—and so he just stopped learning. HA! Gotcha, mom!

WHAT *IS* A MOTHER'S ROLE IN HER CHILD'S EDUCATION?

So what are we supposed to be doing, then? The schools say it's a team effort of home and school. If my child is struggling, do I turn my back and say, "tough?"

No.

Let me outline some of the ways mothers can participate in their children's schooling.

DO

- Do take a real and authentic interest in what your kids are learning at school (but watch that you are not badgering or prying).
- Do keep in touch and be involved with your children's school life by being an active member in the school community. Take time to get to know their teachers and friends. Go to the school performances or maybe book off work for a day each year to help out on a field trip.

- Do set up an appointment for a parent–teacher meeting *that includes your child*, so all three of you can feel like a team working cooperatively to help the child establish and reach her own learning goals for the year.
- Do let your children know that you are there to help but not to take over. Say, "I'm happy to help clarify something if you get stuck, but I have things to do too, so I am not available to sit with you while you do your work. Come find me if you have a question." You don't need to be hostage to homework hour. You'll end up fighting and sticking your nose in if you're sitting right there, anyway!
- Do notice effort and improvement, not perfection: "Wow, all that clarinet practicing is really paying off!"
- Do see mistakes as opportunities to learn: "I'm sorry you're disappointed with your mark on that assignment. What do you think happened? What mark would you like to get on your next one? What do you think you need to do to pull that off next time? Sounds like you have it figured out—I'm sure you'll do it! Let me know if I can be of help."
- Do have faith in your children to accomplish what they would like to, in their way, and in their own time.

DON'T

- Don't label your children (e.g., "he's our scholar"). It adds pressure, devalues them, and discourages siblings from learning.
- Don't give money for good grades (rewards have been proven to reduce motivation).
- Don't make your involvement in the school one of opposition. When you talk badly about the school, the teachers, or the education system, children adopt your attitudes.

- Don't be the calendar, watchdog, and reminder service for your children's school commitments.
- Don't correct your child's work before it is submitted. Of course, everyone would get straight A's if they handed in precorrected papers! Why not go write their tests for them, too?
- Don't get all "woo-woo!" excited about an A. When you do, you're also sending the message that a B is not okay. Simply ask them how they feel about their report card and then LISTEN. Be happy for them!
- Don't take it upon yourself to be your child's tutor. If your child needs extra help, take this up with the teacher.

THE DIRTY SECRET AT THE HEART OF THE EDUCATION MYTHS

"I just want them to be happy."

Sure you do. But many mothers have a tremendously difficult time giving up on these myths, even when they understand how detrimental their over-involvement is. Why? Because there is an ugly truth that we don't like to admit. These myths are by nature classist. Let's face it. In this context, when we say we want our children to be happy, the subtext is that happiness comes from getting an education so you can get a good job and have a good salary, prestige, and the comforts of an upper-middle-class lifestyle.

Did you notice that the "famous dropouts" list (see page 180) names people who all went on to notoriety of some sort? But what of the dropouts who have no "fame," except to their own families and communities?

> ## Totally *Unfamous* High School Dropouts
> - *Robert (grade nine education): opened a lawn-maintenance business, is a dedicated father of two, and is a volunteer fireman for his town. He loves to tinker in his workshop.*

- *Christina (grade 10 education): started a lending library for seniors and drives the book mobile in her town—she can't get her nose out of book!*
- *Anita (grade nine education): sings in the church choir, teaches Sunday school, and is passionate about history. She spends her free time working to trace the family lineage.*

Robert, Christine, and Anita are all somebody's child, too. Many people have lives that are human works of art that do not require academic A's, and they are happy and fulfilled. Believe it or not, scholastic excellence is not a prerequisite to happiness, and we need to stop acting like it's a passport to a better life. Happiness comes from feelings of love, acceptance, belonging, and community. If our true goal is our children's happiness, we need not pressure them to perform—we need to encourage them to be of use to their fellow man.

HOW WE CAN ENCOURAGE CHILDREN

"A child needs encouragement as a plant needs sun and water."
—Dr. Rudolph Dreikurs

Encouragement is the most important aspect of childrearing. The essence of encouragement is to increase children's confidence in themselves, and to convey that *they are good enough* as they are, and not just as they might be.

It is all too common to find that our homes, classrooms, and communities provide a series of discouraging experiences to many children, and that encouragement is given only to those who need it the least. Parents, teachers, and all those who deal with children can keep in mind the following suggestions (these apply in all human relationships):

1. *Avoid discouragement.* The feelings of inferiority that all humans experience must be overcome if we are to function optimally.
2. *Work for improvement, not perfection.* This goes for adults too!
3. *Commend effort.* One's efforts are more significant than one's results.
4. *Separate the deed from the doer.* One may reject the child's actions without rejecting the child.
5. *Show your trust in the child.* This must be sincere, so one must first learn to trust the child.
6. *Do not view mistakes as failures.* We need to take away the stigma of failure. Failure usually indicates a lack of skill. One's worth is not dependent on success.
7. *Remember: failure and defeat will only stimulate special effort when there remains the hope of eventual success.* They do not simulate a deeply discouraged child who has lost all hope of succeeding
8. *Remember, genuine happiness comes from self-sufficiency.* Children need to learn to take care of themselves. Integrate the child into the group rather than treating them as "something special." Treating the child as "something special" increases over-ambition. An overly ambitious child who cannot succeed will usually develop the private logic "If I can't be the best, I'll at least be the worst." Even more seriously, the child may give up altogether.

9. *Stimulating competition usually does not encourage children.* Those who see hope of winning may put forth an extra effort, but the stress is on winning rather than on contribution and cooperation. The less competitive one is, the better one is able to stand competition.

10. *Remember that praise is not the same as encouragement.* Praise may have an encouraging effect on some children, but praise often discourages and causes anxiety and fear. Some come to depend on praise and will perform only for recognition in ever-increasing amounts. Success accompanied by special results-oriented praise may make the child fear "I can never do it again."

11. *Help the child develop the courage to be imperfect.* We all need to learn to take mistakes in stride, and to learn from them.

12. *Don't give responsibility and significance only to those who are already responsible.* Giving opportunities to be responsible to children who are discouraged may make it worthwhile for them to cooperate.

Source: Adapted from my grandmother Edith A. Dewey's article entitled "How We Can Encourage Children," which appeared in resource pages of *The NASAP Newsletter*.

If we can work everyday to incorporate these principles into our relationships, we can move people out of a state of discouragement and into a state of feeling encouraged:

Discouraged	Encouraged
"I can't ..."	"I can ..."
Motivated by others giving them attention	Self-motivated
Looks for power over others	Cooperates
Ego-focused: what's in it for me?	Task-centered: what needs to be done?
Façade	Authentic
Perfectionism, rigidity	Courage to risk and make mistakes
Closed-minded	Open-minded
Retreats from life's challenges	Goes forward and grows
Avoids responsibility by blaming and excusing	Takes personal responsibility
Lack of confidence, feelings of inadequacy	Confident, courageous
Thoughts of worthlessness	Self-respect

Source: Adapted from *Turning People On: How to be an Encouraging Person* by Lewis E. Losoney, 2000 (InSync Press).

ENCOURAGEMENT IS NOT PRAISE

Often people confuse encouragement and praise. Praise is very, very different. Praise is a verbal reward. It is part of the autocratic system of ruling from above, using reward and punishment as tools for controlling underlings. The reward of praise is received only after a task is successfully completed and deemed worthy of the reward.

Encouragement has no interest in the judgment of perfection and completion—it is only interested in the efforts of trying. Encouragement values the person who puts in effort. Encouragement values the improvement that stick-to-it-iveness creates! We must mistake our way to mastery, so let's put our excitement on those who are willing to persist, put out effort, try, make many mistakes, and move forward. *That* is noteworthy and should be appreciated.

THE SPECIAL LANGUAGE OF ENCOURAGEMENT

Phrases that demonstrate acceptance
- "I like the way you handled that."
- "I like the way you tackle a problem."
- "I'm glad you enjoy learning."
- "I am glad you are pleased with it. "
- "Since you are not satisfied, what do you think you can do so that you will be pleased with it?"
- "It looks as if you enjoyed that."
- "How do you feel about it?"

Phrases that show confidence
- "Knowing you, I'm sure you'll do fine."
- "You'll make it."
- "I have confidence in your judgment."
- "That's a rough one, but I am sure you'll work it out."
- "You'll figure it out."

Phrases that focus on contributions, assets, and appreciation
- "Thanks; that helped a lot."
- "It was thoughtful of you to _____."
- "Thanks, I really appreciate _____, because it makes my job easier."
- "I need your help on _____."
- To a family group: "I really enjoyed today. Thanks."
- "You have skill in _____. Would you do that for the family?"

Phrases that recognize improvement
- "It looks as if you really worked hard on that."
- "It looks as if you spent a lot of time thinking that through."
- "I see that you're moving along."
- "Look at the progress you've made." (Be specific, tell how.)
- "You're improving in _____." (Be specific.)
- "You may not feel that you've reached your goal, but look at how far you've come!"

Source: Adapted from resource pages of *The NASAP Newsletter*.

Today's good mothers are surrounded by the message that children should be enriched: that it is not enough to be the way they are. In order to be a good mother today, we must do whatever we can to maximize our children's potential. We are somehow delinquent if we let things unfold along a natural time line. We fear they will fall behind. This is especially true for procuring a good education. We good mothers feel it is our job to raise a family scholar that everyone can feel proud of. This is the crowning accomplishment of motherhood.

We go to perverse lengths to tap in to our children's budding in-tellects and then we ride their backs to ensure academic excellence. Instead of reaching our goal of raising bright learners who enjoy gaining knowledge, we inadvertently judge, pressure, and convey the message that their worth is determined by their achievements. This is a discouraging situation for children, and discouragement is the enemy of learning!

When we learn how to be an encouraging parent, we take the longer view. We can have faith that every human is wired to want to grow, but not always in a linear fashion, or in a way that we can recognize clearly in the moment. If we can encourage and develop in our children a sense of their own worth so firmly fixed that nothing can alter it, no failure rattle it, then we have set the groundwork for them to take life head-on, and to enjoy without fear all that life has to offer.

CHAPTER 8

MYTH:
GOOD MOTHERS MAKE LIFE FUN AND ENTERTAINING

GOOD MOTHERS MAKE LIFE FUN AND ENTERTAINING

T his last myth is particularly insidious because it masquer-
ades as fun-loving, easygoing motherhood. After all, wasn't
that why you picked up this book in the first place? To get rid of
your mothering insanity, presumably replacing it with fun, joy,
and happiness? You probably cracked into this book knowing that
you had some "control" issues, or that you needed better ways of
dealing with conflict. Somehow we accepted those shortcomings.
But who is courageous enough to admit that sometimes it's a fake
smile you paste on while painting cat whiskers on your daughter's
cheek, hiding your more honest grimace? "If I don't even enjoy the
fun parts of motherhood, maybe I shouldn't be a mother at all!"

Not true.

This last myth has been eaten—hook, line, and sinker—by the
masses and we're all paying dearly for it, and this time I really do
mean *pay*, as your credit card statement will attest. Does happiness really have to compound at 20 percent interest per month?
Let's wrap up our myth-busting journey by looking at how we got
oversold on having a fun and entertained family, and invite you
to have a happy, connected family instead.

IT'S ALL ABOUT FUN AND ENTERTAINING, ISN'T IT?

You may not be aware of the societal pressure of being a fun and
entertaining mom until you try to step against the grain. Only then
can you appreciate the incredible force this myth has:

- *Try NOT being a "fun" mom.* The whole world can't be
  the flaming creative extroverted type. When your neighbors have spent hundreds of dollars and a week of labor
  to outfit their house for Halloween—complete with a
  graveyard, stuffed dead corpses hanging from trees, and
  dry ice—while your house has a single carved pumpkin
  and a witch stenciled on the window ... you just know
  your kids are pining to move in next door.

- *Try NOT enjoying time spent playing with your children.* You feel like a pathetic failure of a mother when you tell your kids you don't want to give them a horsie ride around the living room on your back, or you refuse to ride on the back of the toboggan with them.
- *Try NOT consuming at the rate the world has come to expect.* One common television set to share amongst an entire family with only basic cable somehow makes you a modern oddity. Try this same arrangement with a teenager. Now you are both an oddity *and* a villain.

MEET MOM-U-TAINMENT

Long gone are the days when moms kicked their kids out of the house, telling them to go play with the pinecones in the backyard. After all, mom had housework to do. She didn't want children underfoot making a mess for goodness sake! Get outside and play!

But things have changed. We've become "mom-u-tainment" for our children. We've taken it upon ourselves to become our children's full-time playmate and constant companion. The mom-u-tainment mom is a fun-loving gal-pal who takes her place down on the floor amid the Lego, playing gleefully all day long with her children. She's a regular MacGyver, too—turning egg cartons into caterpillars, coffee filters into butterflies.

Every moan of "I'm bored" or "play with me" is answered; tears shed in protest of being left alone are quickly remedied.

But just how much *do* you enjoy having a four-year-old as your "best friend"? Did you get your MBA so you could play Barbies for six hours a day? We're meant to be enjoying this. But are we? It shouldn't be shocking news that you're bored playing a game that says "suitable for ages five to seven" right on the box.

Yet, we still feel lousy about ourselves, even when we're saying "No" to the fifth request to play dress-up since breakfast. Isn't it okay *not* to be the "make-believe-princess-wearing-a-plastic-tiara-while-

hiding-behind-the-couch-safe-from-the-fire-breathing-dragon"
kind of mom? This generation doesn't seem to think so.

The good mother is "it" for tag, a never-ender for skipping, and
sits in the dirt dutifully filling buckets with rocks. Simply supervis-
ing from the sidelines with a coffee and magazine feels like we're
copping out. And when our youngster yells, "did you see, did you
see!" and we realize we actually missed her newest proud feat of
making it all the way across the beam, we feel we've cheated her
of her due attention!

I know not everyone is a mom-u-tainment mom. Some have
made peace with the fact that they're just *not* going to be a veritable "fun factory" of a mother, but they can certainly make up for
any fun that might be lacking by opening up their wallets! Now
that most families are dual-income earners (and mom's salary is
no longer something to sneeze at) we can pride ourselves on being an affluent group of very well-groomed consumers. We like
to spend—especially on our children—and believe me, there are
more offerings of fun and entertainment than you could fit into
one childhood, anyway.

You can take them to the make-your-own-teddy-bear store, and
then pick up the tab for lunch at the Rainforest Café (where the
moving, life-sized elephants will either thrill your tot or make him
shriek in pure terror). There's the inside play-palace, clay painting, or just grab a movie and go an hour early so you can play in
the "midway" first. Ah, yes, every day is a spectacular fun-day in
childhood now.

Shannon spots a new display of water guns—a big honking
"pump-action water-blaster super-soaker CPS 1200" that
claims to shoot water 50 feet. Shannon knows her boys would
just eat those up! They've been missing their dad, who is away
on business, and the soakers are on sale … hmm. Shannon
throws two into her cart. Besides, new toys will keep them

busy outside for hours, and they'll be less likely to fight and bother her while she's parenting alone this week. That's worth the price tag!

Shannon's thinking is pretty commonplace. New toys make our children so happy, keeps them entertained, and—come on, doesn't it make us feel they might just love us that much more? Well, it can't hurt. Why should we restrict the giving of gifts to birthdays and holidays, anyway? If we can afford it, why wait? We've got new toys blowing into our houses on a weekly basis now. They're nothing more than a kiddy consumable that requires replacing. We pick 'em up at the store on the way home from work with the same ease and regularity as we do diapers and milk. Toys are a US$22-billion-a-year business now. Why build a rickety fort with a bed sheet when you can buy a prefab plastic one for only $249? If the slinky gets tangled, no fear—we'll replace it on the weekend.

Oh, Oh, OH! But if Jake mistreats the slinky, if he *dares* throw it uncaringly in a heap, if he disrespects his property with a care-free, don't-give-a-damn, "mom-will-just-by-me-a-new-one-on-the-weekend" attitude (true as it may be), *then* moms start seeing red. I can already hear the "You are so ungrateful" and "That is so disrespectful" lecture that will be delivered.

We're fearful of creating spoiled children, so it's important to us that they do care for and appreciate the things we buy for them. It becomes a value we protect. So, what do we do? The same thing we moms do around *anything* we value highly: OVERDO. Whatever the value (being appreciative, having manners, being sociable, having a good work ethic), if it's really important to mom, she'll be watching closely for it. If mom even suspects her child is act-ing in an unappreciative manner, she pounces to correct for this slight infraction. And she doesn't make a slight correction, she comes down like a hammer.

This overdoing—watching too closely, acting too quickly, and responding too harshly—makes us feel like we are doing our motherly job very well, but it also teaches our children what triggers us. If you want to upset mom, just show a little disrespect to some toy or a lack of appreciation for something she's given you, and then stand back and watch the fireworks! So, in this ironic twist, those parents who most worry about their children having an "attitude" develop it in them! We've already seen how controlling moms end up with uncontrollable kids, and how moms who hate conflict end up with kids who fight. It's because we overdo in our responses that we invite our children to manifest in that very aspect.

And, like our foremothers, we don't want the kids lollygagging about the house—not so much for fear of their making a mess as our concern with idleness. However, we don't kick them out to the yard. We enroll them in exciting programs that are fun (and enriching)—swimming lessons, Karate, art club, soccer, skating, horse riding, dance, and so forth. There's something going on pretty near every evening of the week.

The result is that there really is no idle, downtime for children anymore. Even the car ride to those lessons is made entertaining by watching a movie, thanks to drop-down DVD players. On-board movies have just been added to grocery carts too, mesmerizing your wiggly toddler and allowing you to shop an average of 20 minutes longer! That's a big financial win for food retailers. Portable Game Boys, MP3 players, games on cell phones—all these devices mean that entertainment is eternally at the modern-day child's fingertips. No more misbehavior in restaurants and church pews—just whip out one of these puppies and your child can be quietly entertained through any lull or activity he doesn't enjoy.

THE HIDDEN COST OF FUN

Having fun, spending money, and entertaining children are not problems in and of themselves. But as with all the other myths we've been cracking apart, we simply share a common misunderstanding and then go at our mistaken approaches in an overly ambitious style.

Let me break apart this one last myth by sharing with you the hidden cost of raising children the fun and exciting way that commonly accompanies the modern, fast-parenting approach.

Boredom Is Beautiful—Don't Rescue Them!

Yes, I do think boredom is a beautiful thing for children to experience. If they don't, I end up receiving e-mails like this one:

> *Alyson: My child is three-and-a half years old and 1 can't get anything done because she always has to be with me, or demands that 1 play with her. 1 feel guilty if 1 don't, but 1 am tired of this ball-and-chain on my leg. When is it okay for me to let her play alone?*

This question is a common one. When is it okay? It's "okay" from day one! Children who have a mom that is a constant playmate come to *expect* that she will continue to always be a playmate. Why wouldn't they? It's all they know, and all they have experienced. These children become demanding and dependent. In short, we have overparented, overindulged, and pampered yet again.

In our overdoing style, we inadvertently rob our children of learning to self-entertain. They *need* to see that mom is not always available, and that their own happiness is self-generated from within. It is THEIR job to find and make fun for themselves. They have to learn *how* to self-entertain, and they can only learn by practicing.

This is more important than it first sounds. Boredom and the doldrums are the birthplace of creativity and problem solving. Aren't those lovely qualities to nurture in our children? To do that we have to step back and go the slow route. When we're fed up of listening to our children's moaning mantra of "I am SOOOOO bored" or "plaaaayyy with me," the quick fix of stepping in and playing with them, giving them ideas of what to do with themselves next, or just throwing on a video (even though we said only one hour per day) only solves the problem in the short term.

But, if we could just stand back, wait, wait, wait, wait, … we would see that at the depths of boredom, when the moans are the loudest, the creative spark *will* be ignited! As my husband Ken tells our girls: "You're bored? That's great! Boredom is the moment before inspiration."

Joshua is alone in the backseat of the car. He is bored. He has nothing to do. After ten minutes of fussing and mild complaints, he leans his head back on the seat and notices he can see out the back window. It looks cool watching all the overhead signs pass by. They whoosh by so unexpectedly. Each time is another surprise. He has never stopped to look at the world this way. After ten minutes he spices it up a bit by making guesses about what'll he see next: sign or hydro wire? Eventually he starts to notice that the hydro wires are equidistance apart, and thinks maybe there is some way to measure them. He begins counting between sightings to see.

Joshua has to fill the time, and he knows it. He goes about finding ways, and they stimulate his brain and are very creative. He is paying attention, focused, fully present, thinking, and inquisitive. All this from that blissful state of "boredom."

Play is *very* important to children. But "unstructured free play" is not the same as structured play or being entertained—the growing norm in most families. Unstructured free play is the way children learn. Playing is the "work" of childhood. When children don't have clear set of instructions but are left to create and explore—they will. Discovering that couch cushions can become a fort is creative. It's a new way to look at something. It's outside-the-box thinking. Then the child may discover how you have to work to balance them on end, which is itself a lesson in science. Think of the multitude of things you learned to do with those crumbly little brown pinecones! Pluck them apart, see if they bounce, try interlocking them, make a game out of throwing them at a target. If you're the child coming up with this stuff, your brain is on fire! But if you're just the playmate of mom, and she invents the pinecone toss game, it becomes structured play again. It's the creation that's most important.

I observed a great example of the power of non–adult-directed, free, unstructured play one day at a nursery school. A group of girls had made their way to the kitchen area and were playing house. Another group of boys were playing with the block set. What happened next was the workings of two social groups trying to figure out how to play together. One boy grabbed some of the plastic food from the girls and ran it back to the boys' block area. He put the food in the little corral they had built with blocks. The girls ran and snatched it back. After a few more rounds of robbing one another, which they did chuckling—having fun being sneaky and trying to outwit each other—they combined their games. All the food went to the boys who used the blocks to set up a food market, and the girls came to shop with their imaginary grocery carts.

They learned about cooperation and socializing: When is stealing and snatching "fun" and when is it stepping over the line? How can you get someone to play with you? How can you turn two games into one? How can blocks be used as food storage?

So many things to learn! And this is the format to do it—experientially. Imagine now if the typical mom was on the scene. I promise you, one of those children would have been disciplined for not sharing, or sent to a time-out for taking the plastic food without asking. There would have been the lecture on why stealing is wrong. Mom would have solved the dilemma of two teams wanting the plastic fruits by dividing them up and making a mental note to buy more plastic play fruit. All of that would have interrupted the flow of this lovely game, and ruined the wise learning that took place. These are exactly the kinds of experiences that our children need more of, and that means less you.

The other beautiful thing about allowing our children to experience "boredom" is that it allows them to realize boredom is a subjective state of being: we can be bored and agitated in the moment, or we can enjoy the slower tempos of life. Joshua made the switch himself in the car. Next time he finds himself "killing time," he'll remember how he turned things around for himself by enjoying the passing of signs. It's a choice! Nothing is inherently boring. It is your creation of the moment and how you interpret it that matters. We need to teach our children that lesson as much as we need to learn it ourselves.

Time Lost

I would like to point out some general trends that may not be on your radar.

It seems when they are little, we can barely give our children a moment to themselves, but when they get older we hand them off willy-nilly. Most older children today spend the vast majority of their time in the presence of adults *other than their own mom and dad*. They have their teachers at school all day, and then a coach or instructor in the evening. Time studies show that most of the time kids *do* spend with their parents involves getting them ready, out of the house, and shuttled around to these programs. Mom as mentor is quickly being replaced with mom as chauffeur. Now, I don't know about your particular house, but let me tell ya, in my experience, nothing invites more squabbles and yelling than a mom trying to get her children to their commitments on time. It's a daily scene that most of us think of as the low point in our day. Sad to think this is how we spend the majority of our time with our older children.

Also worth taking stock of is our society's alarming trend toward a decline in the amount of family communication. If you were to record a family's interactions and count the actual number of words spoken, you'd see it is on the decline compared to past generations. That car ride to soccer used to be a time to talk, but now the kids are watching *Harry Potter* DVDs. The family used to play cards and board games, which invited friendly banter, but now we largely spend our time watching TV together, talking only briefly at the commercials.

Conversations are an important part of relationship building that's eroding, being pushed out by MP3s and portable gadgets that fill the time that might otherwise have been filled with chatter.

I am by no means old-fashioned. My house is wired for everything, and I love using new technologies, but I think it's time we thought more consciously about how our time is spent and the balance we have in our family lives. When we say "yes" to an activity, what are we saying "no" to? We all make choices, but often it's the default path we take, with little thought and no clear intention. If we want more time together as a family because we value closeness and connection, then perhaps staying home to play cards IS the better alternative to a skiing holiday where everyone ends up on different hills. Given how precious your time is, maybe taking your children to the pool for family swim time is a better choice than passively viewing their swimming lessons from the pool gallery. Only you can decide how best to slice up your family time—I only ask you to make it a considered decision.

The Cost to Us Financially

I started by saying we have more affluence than ever before, but we are also the most in debt. It's hard to believe that credit cards are only an invention of the 1960s. In very short order they became a key part in changing our spending habits. We use them heavily, and we are VERY comfortable carrying debt. We have never lived through a stock market crash, a depression, or a world war. Our experience is that life is good! We'll go into debt if it means making a good life for our children—we want to make sure they don't go without. Now, let me clarify that. Going "without" in the old days meant being shoeless. Oh, no—we're playing in a much bigger arena now. When our generation wants to be sure our kids don't miss out on the "basics," that includes Nike runners, personal TVs in their bedrooms, laptop computers, cell phones, leather jackets, and mountain bikes. Only a few decades ago the typical child received about 50 toys by the time he had celebrated his fifth birthday. In 1995 that number had jumped to 500! What must it be now?

We seem to think that going to Disney World is a "right" of passage, and that by denying our children we are somehow being negligent. Holidays once spent camping at the KOA have been upgraded to Family Club Med in Mexico, and swimming with dolphins in Discovery Cove. This stuff is becoming "standard fare." This is the new "average" family holiday.

But there's one small hitch: none of us can afford it!

Besides being the "fun-loving" demographic, we could also be known collectively as the "consuming beyond our means" demographic. We've created a middle-class standard of living that is well above what most middle-class people can financially afford. Most of us are in debt 120 percent of our annual income. Because family finances are thought to be of a private nature, no one is talking about the taboo subject of money and debt. If everyone else on the block can afford private school, shouldn't you? If all the other kids at school have their own computer for doing homework, shouldn't your kids? Seems we're tongue-tied when it comes to saying, "I can't afford this."

SLOW PARENTING YOUR WAY TO HAPPINESS

We all want the same thing for our children and families. Happiness. So elusively simple, isn't it?

Our mom-u-tainment approach is a frenetic attempt at providing our children with an idyllic "happy childhood." We've invested a huge amount of our precious time and drained our bank accounts in an effort to secure their happiness, pour it into them somehow, but our tactics and execution are misguided.

Sure, a mom can make her children laugh and distract them from boredom, but she can't truly make them happy. That's their job to do. Happiness comes from within. It's not so much a goal as a byproduct of our actions. It's the children themselves who must be active agents in the making of their happiness.

> *"We survive here in dependence on others. Whether we like it or not, there is hardly a moment of our lives when we do not benefit from others' activities. For this reason it is hardly surprising that most of our happiness arises in the context of our relationships with others."*
>
> —*The Dalai Lama*

That happiness comes from feeling a great sense of connection with others, and from being in rich relationships where we feel we belong and are needed. These rich, caring relationships fuel our soul. When we give back, we feel closer to others. When we feel closer, we want to give back more: the cycle winds us in tighter, and we just keep getting happier! But it takes time. Relationships, like aging wine and simmering robust stews, require slow nurturance and savoring. They are ruined by speed. It is in their nature to be slow and deep. Take your time building fortifying lifelong relationships with your children.

So, while moms can't "make" their children happy, they can do their part in creating a family culture that values and nurtures happiness. The self-care we discussed earlier in this book can sat-

GOOD MOTHERS MAKE LIFE FUN AND ENTERTAINING

isfy our first duty: to be happy ourselves. What a lovely responsibility to have.

> *"There is no duty we so underrate as the duty of being happy. By*
> *being happy we sow anonymous benefits upon the world."*
>   —*Robert Louis Stevenson*

We can also create homes that are lovingly unhurried and
unpressured so that, just maybe, just maybe—something creative and interesting might have a chance to develop and grow.
Think wisely about how you choose to spend your time. Make
it a conscious decision. Does your calendar reflect your values?
Are you spending time doing those things you care most about?
Are you leaving enough time for the wonder of "nothingness,"
to see what grows in that fallow field? Can you find that balance
between consta-playmate and chauffeur? Can you live by your
values without "overdoing," so they don't backfire and get rejected by your children?

We can try a new kind of experience in our families; instead of
outsourcing all the work and only sharing leisure and entertainment, try building family connectivity and happiness through
facing a common challenge and toiling together. Paint a room
together; start a vegetable garden together; even the communal
work of planning that trip to Disney World—if done together—
is a bonding experience because everyone is working towards a
common goal. Hopefully, your family meetings will have already
proven some of this to you.

You can also teach (and practice) human connectedness through
establishing family traditions and rituals. What childhood traditions were special for you? What traditions would your family like
to consciously build together? Everyone spending an evening to-

gether in front of the TV, cheering for your favorite team on *The Amazing Race*, can be a family ritual.

Go ahead and play that video game together, take the whole crew out bowling and—if you can do it—zoom off to swim with the dolphins. And on a rainy Wednesday evening, when the clouds are low-hanging and the whole family wishes they could be somewhere else, why not try the impossible: do nothing together! Wait for the magic! *Someone* will come up with *something* fun—and your kids will learn not only how powerful their imaginations are, but also the quiet, profound joy of being truly close with someone they love: Mom!

CONCLUSION

Human change takes time, and I recognize that one book is not going to instantaneously alter a lifetime of patterns. You have only just begun to unpack the private logic of your own mind. But you've begun!

I hope I have managed to break some of your "good mother" myths. In fact, the entire idea of seeking out motherly perfection should seem preposterous to you now. "Perfect? Who's perfect? What an illusion! Ha! What a superior attitude!"

Let's leave it behind us, shall we?

You are—and will always be—wonderfully imperfect. In this very moment, you are just fine "as is." In all these pages, if you have come to accept *that one singular point*, you are poised to achieve greatness for yourself and your children. Congratulations for having the courage to be imperfect!

I've introduced you to the Adlerian perspective on human nature and child guidance. I hope it excited you enough to want to learn more. I've seen people have a revelatory experience when they learn this information—moms bursting free of the shackles of these myths, with a new clear vision of what they need to do. But concepts like social equality, true encouragement, being noncompetitive, and learning to strive positively, well—they are big ideas. Much like the ancient Chinese board game "Go," they are beautifully simple and easy to teach, but they can take years and years to master.

Don't get discouraged with the journey. There was not a single chapter I wrote that didn't cause me to stop and review my own life. In fact, in a few of these points I have made a *complete* hypocrite of myself. But, as Adler himself wrote: "It is easier to fight for our principles than to live by them." And so, I plough on with my own work of living by these principles as best as I can, including forgiving myself for my shortcomings. I encourage you to do the same!

> *"Courage is not the absence of fear, but rather the judgment that something else is more important than fear."*
>
> —*Ambrose Redmoon*

If you want to join other like-minded moms who have read this book or have taken my courses, join our online community at **www. alyson.ca**, where you can post your questions and read hundreds of tips and techniques for implementing democratic discipline. We all need to continue to learn on this front, and staying connected to other mothers working on similar issues will help you feel supported as you grow your family into the one you envision.

Is Adler's way the "right" way? Well, I am not so concerned with its "correctness." I purposely choose to accept this philosophy as the guiding force of my life. I do believe people are basically good and that only discouragement can ruin us. I believe we all need to be in loving and accepting communities. I believe that with proper child guidance we can steer our children away from self-interested competition and conflict and help them to move toward nurturing those same communities cooperatively.

I also believe that raising children is a most challenging task, one that does not get the respect it deserves. If we want humanity to thrive peacefully as families, communities, and nations, it must start one small child at a time. There is no greater lesson a child can learn than the skill of cooperation—to be able to live and thrive amongst others communally. If we can guide our children toward useful contribution and keep them encouraged, treating them with the respect and dignity they deserve, our next generation will lock arms together and soar!

ACKNOWLEDGEMENTS

'd like to thank my grandparents Edith and Milton Dewey, who first met Dr. Rudolph Dreikurs through his lectures, and who then became very involved in the North American Society for Adlerian Psychology. My parents, Sylvia Dewey Knight and Richard Knight, who also conducted Adlerian parent study classes, and who raised me and my three older brothers according to these principles. If it had not been for these early introductions to this philosophy, I would not have followed this enlightened path.

Thanks also to all my many teachers who have helped me to understand Adler's work and who have encouraged me to spread his message far and in my own style; Althea Poulos, Larry Nisan, Linda Page, Richard Kopp, Leo Lobel, Drs. Joyce and Gary McKay, Daniel Eckstein and Erik Mansager.

Thanks also to Wiley for presenting me with the opportunity to write this book, most especially my editor Leah Fairbank, who went way above the call of duty in working with me as a new writer. In fact, the whole Wiley team got behind this book and made it come alive.

I would also like to recognize those people who shepherded me along: Liza Findlay, Julie Weiss, Joanne Flynn, Colette Annetts, Connie Runions and my husband Ken Schafer and our children Zoe and Lucy. Your support meant everything to me.

To Amy Halpenny of The Ella Centre, who offered up her centre for me to talk to mothers about their experiences, and indeed my own coaching clients and course graduates whose stories I drew on for content.

"There is no task too big if it is a common task."

—*Alfred Adler*